Other Kaplan Success with English Words Books

Success with Business Words

Success with Legal Words

Success with Medical Words

Success with Words for the TOEFL

Other Kaplan Books on Related Topics

Access America's Guide to Studying in the U.S.A.

Guide to College Selection

Kaplan Word Power

Kaplan Grammar Power

Kaplan/Newsweek Business School Admissions Adviser

Kaplan/Newsweek Graduate School Admissions Adviser

TOEFL

TOEIC

Success with
American Idioms

By Lin Lougheed and the
Staff of Kaplan Educational Centers

Simon & Schuster

Kaplan Books
Published by Kaplan Educational Centers and Simon & Schuster
1230 Avenue of the Americas
New York, NY 10020

Project Editor: Julie Schmidt
Cover Design: Cheung Tai
Interior Page Design: Michael Shevlin
Production Editor: Maude Spekes
Desktop Publishing Manager: Michael Shevlin
Managing Editor: Brent Gallenberger
Executive Editor: Del Franz
Executive Director, International Products and Programs:
Marilyn J. Rymniak

Special thanks to Amy Arner Sgarro, Enid Burns, Alison May, and
Pamela Vittorio

Manufactured in the United States of America
Published simultaneously in Canada

July 1998

10 9 8 7 6 5 4 3 2 1

Library of Congress Cataloging in Publication Data

Lougheed, Lin, 1946–
    Success with American idioms / by Lin Lougheed, and the staff
of Kaplan Educational Centers.
        p.   cm.
    ISBN 0-684-85402-3
    1. English language--Textbooks for foreign speakers. 2. English
language--United States--Idioms--Problems, exercises, etc.
3. English language--Examinations--Study guides. I. Kaplan
Educational Centers (Firm: New York, N.Y.) II. Title.
PE1128.L654 1998
428.2'4--dc21   98-29736
                                                     CIP

ISBN 0-684-85402-3

Table of Contents

How to Use this Book

If you've studied English, you know that after you've reached a certain level, you need to work on refining and improving your vocabulary. As you become more familiar with the English language, you want to be able to use and understand the same sophisticated, idiomatic vocabulary as your American classmates or colleagues.

Success with American Idioms is an invaluable tool for student or professional nonnative speakers of English seeking to master everyday, idiomatic American English. It uses a variety of methods to help you to incorporate 450 idioms, mostly phrasal verbs, into your vocabulary. Many phrasal verbs vary in meaning according to the context in which they are used, and may appear in more than one chapter.

Each of the 30 chapters in this book focuses on words or phrases that are related to a particular theme, such as *At a Hotel* or *Relationships*. Each chapter offers three different types of exercises that encourage you to contextualize and actively use these words or phrases. The first exercise consists of two columns in which 15 words or phrases listed in the left-hand column are to be matched with the correct definitions in the right-hand column. You should try to see how many phrases and meanings you can match up without using your dictionary. If this proves difficult, move on to the passages on the second page of the chapter and try reading them aloud to yourself or with a partner. The two conversations and the short talk you will find here use the terms from the matching list in relevant, realistic contexts. Seeing these phrases in their proper context should enable you to go back to the first exercise and match any terms that you were not able to figure out with their meanings.

On the third page of each chapter, there is a fill-in-the-blank exercise that tests your understanding of the 15 words and expressions covered in the chapter. In this exercise you will "recycle" your vocabulary by putting the phrases that you learned in the matching exercise and passages into sentences, contextualizing them further. This will aid you in retaining them as "learned" vocabulary. Be aware that these exercises occasionally ask you to provide the term in a different part of speech or tense than that which is used in the matching list. This encourages you to develop and reinforce a sense of how the term is actively used in conversational English.

After you have completed the fill-in-the-blank exercise, you should review your work and check your answers in the answer keys on the fourth and final page of each chapter. Then read the conversations and short talk one more time to check your comprehension again.

You may work through these chapters in sequence, or by topic of interest. You can also look up unfamiliar phrases in the index and do the exercises that center around them. Whichever method you choose, you will master commonly used idioms that will improve your fluency in everyday American English.

Good luck and enjoy using this book!

1 Waking Up

Match each word or phrase to its meaning:

1. turn off   remove hair with a blade

2. get up   rotate to opposite side

3. be up to   leave one's bed

4. get out   be activated, sound

5. call in   exit on the run

6. shave off   exit

7. cut off   cause something not to be heard

8. come on!   telephone

9. knock off   remove with scissors

10. go off   return to an earlier condition, position, or action

11. drown out   stop

12. turn over   take off, cause to not be somewhere

13. go back   leave quickly

14. jump out   expressing disbelief, sarcasm

15. run out   in the mood for

Can you figure out the meanings of the italicized words in the following passages?

Conversation One:

VICTOR: *Turn off* the alarm clock. It's too early to *get up.*

FIONA: Rise and shine! It's time to *get out* of bed and get going! You have a full day ahead of you at the office.

VICTOR: I'*m* not *up to* a full day. I'm going to *call in* sick.

Conversation Two:

ANN-MARIE: Why don't you *shave* your beard *off?*

STEVE: I don't think that's a good idea. I might *cut off* a few gray hairs, but I'm too lazy to shave every day.

ANN-MARIE: *Come on.* If you were clean shaven, you'd *knock* ten years *off* your age.

STEVE: Hey, wait a minute! Are you trying to tell me I look old?

Short Talk:

When the alarm clock *goes off,* most people just *turn over,* cover their heads with a pillow to *drown out* the sound, and go back to sleep. Some, however, *jump out of* bed, do a few exercises, take a shower, dress and *run out* of the house. They don't even take time for breakfast.

Fill in the blanks to complete the sentences:

16. _____ you _____ another game of cards, or do you want to go to bed?

17. She wasn't feeling well, so she _____ sick.

18. Close the screen door so the cats don't _____.

19. I'll _____ the radio _____ so it doesn't bother you while you're studying.

20. If the fire alarm _____, call the fire department immediately.

21. I asked the barber not to touch my sideburns, but he went ahead and _____ them _____ anyway.

22. The singer was so loud that she _____ the rest of the band.

23. The salesperson _____ about $10 _____ the retail price.

24. We need to _____ early tomorrow if we're going to be at work by nine.

25. They wanted to leave early, but they couldn't _____ of the office until eight.

26. Oh, _____! You should have known better than that!

27. The pedestrian _____ of the way of the car just in time.

28. One should _____ a mattress every six months.

29. Before you wrap the present, _____ the price tags.

30. I'd like to _____ to bed and catch a little more sleep.

Answer Key

1. stop
2. leave one's bed
3. in the mood for
4. exit
5. telephone
6. remove hair with a blade
7. remove with scissors or a knife
8. expression showing disbelief or sarcasm
9. take away
10. be activated, make a sound
11. cause something not to be heard
12. rotate to opposite side
13. return to an earlier condition, position, or action
14. exit on the run
15. leave quickly

16. are (you) up to
17. called in
18. run out
19. turn (the radio) off
20. goes off
21. shaved (them) off
22. drowned out
23. knocked (about $10) off
24. get up
25. get out
26. come on
27. jumped out
28. turn over
29. cut off
30. go back

2 Getting Ready

Match each word or phrase to its meaning:

1.	look for	enter a house or building
2.	look out	accompany one another
3.	put down	watch out for
4.	come in	trick someone
5.	put someone on	meet; match; be in alignment with
6.	speed up	find; locate
7.	go together	stop holding, set down
8.	put on	throw away
9.	measure up	go faster
10.	walk out	buy; purchase; look for in stores
11.	keep an eye on	leave on foot
12.	take in	place on something
13.	toss out	pick out or select and arrange so as to facilitate something
14.	shop for	shorten the length of or make narrower
15.	lay out	be careful, pay attention

Can you figure out the meanings of the italicized words in the following conversations?

Conversation One:

KAREN: Would you help me *look for* my keys?

PAT: You'll have to learn to *keep an eye on* your own stuff. Do you remember *putting* them *down* anywhere?

KAREN: When I *came in* last night, I thought I had *put* them *on* the table, but they're not there now.

PAT: *Look out*! They're right under your feet!

Conversation Two:

PAT: Could you *speed up* a little? If you're not ready in five minutes, we won't be able to *go together*.

BURT: Hey, it's not easy to match a tie with a shirt.

PAT: I'm sorry your life is so complicated. Perhaps if we had live-in help, they could *lay out* your clothes for you.

BURT: I'd be afraid I wouldn't *measure up* to their high standards, and they would *walk out* the first day.

PAT: You're *putting me on!* You'd love it!

Short Talk:

As fashion changes, it is important to *keep an eye on* the latest trends. If short skirts are stylish, women will want to *take in* the hems of their skirts. If narrow ties are in vogue, men will want to *toss out* the wide ones and *shop for* replacements. Of course, you can always be your own fashion critic and wear whatever you feel like wearing. Let everyone else follow your lead.

Fill in the blanks to complete the sentences:

16. I'll _____ for dinner as soon as I'm done washing the car.

17. I hope I can _____ to the new boss's expectations.

18. Please have the seamstress _____ the hem another inch.

19. I'm hungry—let's _____ a Chinese restaurant for dinner.

20. He's so organized, he always _____ his suits _____ the night before.

21. _____! That truck nearly hit you!

22. If you can finish your work by 6, we'll be able to _____ to the meeting _____.

23. He's always _____ a bargain.

24. Even though the alarm went off, the thief _____ the door without anyone noticing him.

25. We _____ the lawn chairs when they got rusty.

26. Let me just _____ these books _____ and I will help you carry yours.

27. We were told to _____ if we didn't want to work late.

28. He realized his co-workers were _____ him _____ when they all started laughing.

29. When you come in, please _____ the car keys _____ the kitchen counter so I can find them.

30. Monica asked me to _____ her dog while she was on vacation.

Answer Key

1. find; locate
2. be careful, pay attention
3. stop holding, set down
4. enter a house or building
5. trick someone
6. go faster
7. accompany one another
8. place on something
9. meet; match; be in alignment with
10. leave on foot
11. watch out for
12. shorten the length of or make narrower
13. throw away
14. buy; purchase; look for in stores
15. pick out or select and arrange so as to facilitate something
16. come in
17. measure up
18. take in
19. look for
20. lays (his suits) out
21. look out
22. go (to the meeting) together
23. shopping for
24. walked out
25. tossed out
26. put (these books) down
27. speed up
28. putting (him) on
29. put (the car keys) on
30. keep an eye on

Match each word or phrase to its meaning:

1.	put in	go to
2.	pick up	get; buy
3.	turn on	begin
4.	check out	give a ride to some place
5.	run down to	avoid
6.	pick up	make operable; start
7.	mess with	follow; become used to
8.	fool around with	tolerate
9.	put up with	connect to an electrical source
10.	start off with	give
11.	get into	place into
12.	stay away from	annoy
13.	plug in	casually try different things out
14.	rile up	tamper with or change
15.	hand over	look into; investigate

Can you figure out the meanings of the italicized words in the following passages?

Conversation One:

TONY: *Put in* a slice of bread for me, will you?

NADINE: The toaster is full. You'll have to *stand in* line.

TONY: Come on! My ride will be *picking* me *up* any minute. *Hand over* one of your slices.

Conversation Two:

LINDA: What's wrong with this coffee maker? I *turned* it *on,* and nothing's happening.

CLYDE: Maybe it's not *plugged in.* Or maybe you forgot to *put* water *in* the tank.

LINDA: I *checked out* both. I'd better *run down to* the corner and get some coffee from the deli.

CLYDE: Would you mind *picking up* some pastries for me while you're there?

Short Talk:

You can't *mess with* anyone's breakfast. You may be able to surprise someone with a new taste sensation for lunch. You might be able to *fool around* with new ways to prepare chicken for dinner, but at breakfast time, people are not in the mood for experiments. They won't *put up with* different tastes early in the day. Most people *start off* their day *with* the same thing, day after day, week after week, month after month. People *get into* a routine, and if the routine changes, they get *riled up* and will make their anger known. *Stay away* from someone who did not get his normal breakfast.

Fill in the blanks to complete the sentences:

16. I _____ from stores that have a lot of sales staff pestering me to buy things.

17. Elizabeth asked her secretary to _____ her mail _____ the outgoing basket.

18. If no one can _____ the ambassador at three, I'll have a taxi sent for him.

19. When the policeman stopped her, she had to _____ her driver's license to him.

20. Make sure the toaster isn't _____ if you're going to repair it.

21. If he hadn't _____ the computer program, it would probably still be working.

22. We _____ the day _____ with a trip to the beach.

23. If you're going to the grocery store on the corner, please _____ some milk.

24. I'll _____ the bakery and get some doughnuts for breakfast.

25. It is important to quietly _____ a new employee's mistakes and many questions.

26. Maria got _____ when she was not invited to her best friend's engagement party.

27. It used to be easy to _____ a daily exercise program. .

28. _____ these scarves and colors until you find a combination you like.

29. She _____ all her options and decided to invest in the stock market.

30. I usually _____ the TV if I'm home alone.

Answer Key

1. place into
2. give a ride to some place
3. make operable; start
4. look into; investigate
5. go to
6. get; buy
7. tamper with or change
8. casually try different things out
9. tolerate
10. begin
11. follow; become used to
12. avoid
13. connect to an electrical source
14. annoy
15. give
16. stay away
17. put (her mail) in
18. pick up
19. hand over
20. plugged in
21. messed with
22. started (the day) off
23. pick up
24. run down to
25. put up with
26. riled up
27. get into
28. fool around with
29. checked out
30. turn on

4 Going to Work

Match each word or phrase to its meaning:

1.	pull over	push down quickly
2.	make a run for	get into
3.	hop in	head towards quickly
4.	put someone out	turn on, cause to operate
5.	slam on	depend on; decide to
6.	make up one's mind	find the radio frequency of a station
7.	buckle in	inconvenience someone
8.	get off	board quickly
9.	turn off	drive to the side and stop
10.	switch on	grasp
11.	tune in to	be well prepared, be ahead of others
12.	be ahead of the game	swing off one road onto another
13.	plan on	decide
14.	jump on	fasten up
15.	hold on	exit from, leave

Can you figure out the meanings of the italicized words in the following passages?

Conversation One:

DAWN: Hey Lloyd, can you drive me to work today?

LLOYD: Sure, *hop in*! I'll *pull over* to the curb and let you out a couple blocks from your office.

DAWN: I don't want to *put* you *out*, but could we get a little closer? It's raining.

LLOYD: Sorry, it's a one-way street. I think you'll have to *make a run for* it.

Conversation Two:

CARA: Sorry. I didn't mean to *slam on* the brakes, but that driver ahead of me can't *make up his mind* whether he wants to go or stop.

SIMON: No problem. I've *buckled* myself *in*. This traffic is really *backed up*.

CARA: Maybe I'll *turn off* at that exit and take a side road.

SIMON: *Switch on* the radio and *tune into* the traffic report. We might *be ahead of the game* if we stay put.

Short Talk:

Getting to work by bus is always an adventure. If you are in a hurry, you can *plan on* having to wait a long time for the bus. There will always be a lot of traffic that the bus must work its way through. When it finally comes to your stop, you will have to *jump on* and fight your way toward the rear. Since there are no seats, you will have to *hold on* to a strap. The bus is so crowded you can't see out of the window. You just have to hope you will be able to *get off* at the correct stop.

Fill in the blanks to complete the sentences:

16. I'll _____ an express train and get there as soon as I can.

17. We panicked and _____ the exit when someone shouted "Fire!" in the concert hall.

18. To see the countryside, they _____ the highway onto a country road.

19. We _____ at a roadside diner after driving all day.

20. The elderly woman made sure to _____ to the railing as she went up the stairs.

21. This device will automatically _____ the generators if the lights go out.

22. We _____ leaving at six, but we had to reschedule.

23. She didn't want to _____ him _____, so she walked home instead of calling her father for a ride.

24. Make sure all the kids are _____ safely before you drive off.

25. If we make sure to finish all of the reports by five this afternoon, we will be _____.

26. They _____ the train when they realized they were going the wrong way.

27. _____ the local news station, please.

28. We're driving to the beach, so _____ the car if you want to come along.

29. You shouldn't _____ the brakes when you're driving on ice.

30. She'll have to _____ today about purchasing the house.

Answer Key

1. drive to the side and stop
2. head towards quickly
3. get into
4. inconvenience someone
5. push down quickly
6. decide
7. fasten up
8. exit from, leave
9. swing off one road onto another
10. turn on, cause to operate
11. find the radio frequency of a station
12. be well prepared, be ahead of others
13. depend on; decide to
14. board quickly
15. grasp
16. jump on
17. made a run for
18. turned off
19. pulled over
20. hold on
21. switch on
22. planned on
23. put him out
24. buckled in
25. ahead of the game
26. got off
27. tune in to
28. hop in
29. slam on
30. make up her mind

5 At the Office

Match each word or phrase to its meaning:

1. pull up   complete

2. get in   absorb, use

3. fill out   panic, get nervous from too much work

4. depend on   not take along

5. write out   draw near

6. take up   concentrate

7. leave behind   hand over, turn in

8. focus on   eliminate over time

9. mix up   review

10. stress out   check over

11. go over   do something elsewhere

12. phase out   to require something as a necessary condition

13. go out   hand in

14. look over   confuse

15. turn in   fill out, put in writing

Can you figure out the meanings of the italicized words in the following passages?

Conversation One:

PAM: Good morning. *Pull up* a chair and join me in a cup of coffee.

KEN: Thanks, but I have to *get in* these reports before noon.

PAM: You always look so *stressed out*! Don't work so hard!

Conversation Two:

PAM: Would you mind going over these forms with me? I'm so *mixed up*. Are these what I need to *fill out* to order supplies?

KEN: It *depends on* what you need. If you need general office supplies, these forms will do.

PAM: We're *phasing out* our old computers, and we need to *go out* and buy new ones.

KEN: In that case, *write out* a purchase order. I'll *look* it *over* before you *turn* it *in*.

Short Talk:

Many people think of the office as their second home. People are happy at work because they can to some extent control their environment there. At home, they have children doing unpredictable things and *taking up* too much of their time. At work, they can *leave* all the problems of home *behind* them and *focus on* things they can control.

Fill in the blanks to complete the sentences:

16. _____a chair and sit down!

17. I _____ my report on time, but they still haven't given me any feedback.

18. They're _____ this brand of toothpaste, so we should stock up while it lasts.

19. I got _____ when I was given two different sets of instructions to program the printer.

20. Let's _____ increasing the market share of our products.

21. We're _____ you to earn more money; if not, we'll starve.

22. If we can't do the job, we'll have to _____ and hire a consultant.

23. I need to _____ these claims _____ before the deadline.

24. Nancy felt very _____ because of her numerous deadlines.

25. Having forgotten his glasses, Bob asked for some help in _____ the job application.

26. I wasn't able to _____ the check because there wasn't enough money in the account.

27. I _____ your rough draft and I think you need to revise it extensively.

28. We won't _____ any more of your time; we've stayed way too long already.

29. You should _____ the proposal before you submit it to the client.

30. We made sure not to _____ any trash _____ when we left the beach.

Answer Key

1. draw near
2. hand over, turn in
3. complete
4. to require something as a necessary condition
5. fill out, put in writing
6. absorb, use
7. not take along
8. concentrate
9. confuse
10. panic, get nervous from too much work
11. review
12. eliminate over time
13. do something elsewhere
14. check over
15. hand in
16. pull up
17. turned in
18. phasing out
19. mixed up
20. focus on
21. depending on
22. go out
23. get (these claims) in
24. stressed out
25. filling out
26. write out
27. looked over
28. take up
29. go over
30. leave (any trash) behind

6 Lunch Time

Match the word or phrase to its meaning:

1. eat in	take care of, pay
2. eat out	phone
3. call up	buy food from restaurant and take it home
4. send over	deliver
5. whip up	figure out, determine
6. add up to	relax, do at a leisurely pace
7. work out	continue
8. pick up	eat hurriedly
9. be made up of	dine at home
10. wolf down	discover
11. take one's time	come to a total of
12. hurry up	move rapidly
13. get on with	consist of
14. takeout	prepare something quickly
15. come across	eat in a restaurant

Can you figure out the meanings of the italicized words in the following passages?

Conversation One:

ERIC: It's time for lunch. Shall we *eat in* or *eat out*?

MICHELLE: I feel like having Chinese food. Yesterday, I *came across* a *take-out* restaurant near here. We can even *call up* and have it *sent over*.

ERIC: That suits me. Then, I won't have to *whip* something *up*.

Conversation Two:

MICHELLE: The bill *adds up to* $30.42. Shall we just divide it?

ERIC: Fine with me, but I had more to eat than you did.

MICHELLE: Not that much more. Besides, it's too complicated to *work out* what each of us ate.

ERIC: Let me *pick up* the tip then.

Short Talk:

The lunch crowd in a popular restaurant *is made up of* three kinds of people—solitary workers *wolfing down* a quick bite before rushing back to work, shoppers taking a quick break in between stores, and business people trying to close a deal or cement a relationship. The key elements in a popular lunch spot are speed, value, and quality of food, in that order. Many diners constantly urge the wait staff to *hurry up*. They want to *get on with* their day. They do not want to be overwhelmed by a long menu. They want a few select items that they know will be properly priced and tasty. Other diners, on the other hand, prefer to *take their time* and enjoy their meals.

Fill in the blanks to complete the sentences:

16. We'll have to _____ this task if we ever want to finish it.

17. If we _____ a coffee shop, let's stop and have a cup.

18. I know you are in a hurry, but no child of mine is going to _____ his dinner.

19. I had flowers _____ to welcome them to their new home.

20. We decided to _____, since we had been going out every night.

21. She wanted her husband to _____ a cake for the occasion, but he didn't have time.

22. I _____ eating, since I didn't have to be back at the office until much later on.

23. As a salesman, I often _____ with clients.

24. Rather than spend time cooking ourselves, why don't we just get a _____ Indian meal?

25. The accountant _____ that you paid too much in taxes last year.

26. The cost for these four computers _____ about twice what we were expecting to pay.

27. If you don't _____, we'll miss the flight.

28. Mr. Guzman always _____ the bill when we go out.

29. When eating out, I always _____ the restaurant in advance and reserve a table.

30. Our staff _____ hotel school graduates who are highly trained in the service industry.

Answer Key

1. dine at home
2. eat in a restaurant
3. telephone
4. deliver
5. cook food quickly
6. come to a total of
7. figure out, determine
8. take care of, pay
9. consist of
10. eat hurriedly
11. relax, do at a leisurely pace
12. move rapidly
13. continue
14. buy food from restaurant and take it home
15. discover
16. get on with
17. come across
18. wolf down
19. sent over
20. eat in
21. whip up
22. took my time
23. eat out
24. takeout
25. worked out
26. adds up to
27. hurry up
28. picks up
29. call up
30. is made up of

7 On the Telephone

Match each word or phrase to its meaning:

1.	ring off the hook	return
2.	hang up	make an effort to communicate with
3.	call back	end a telephone call
4.	head off for	not be in communication
5.	get in touch	convince
6.	give someone a break	be in communication
7.	get back	little cost for great benefit
8.	put someone on hold	constantly ring
9.	be in touch	stroll along
10.	be out of touch	depart for
11.	walk down	depend on something happening with certainty
12.	small price to pay	complete
13.	finish up	return a call
14.	talk into	make one caller wait while you talk with someone else or do another task
15.	bank on	make things easier for someone

Can you figure out the meanings of the italicized words in the following passages?

Conversation One:

KIM: That phone has been *ringing off the hook* all morning. Just as I *finish up* with one call, I get another. Can't these people *give me a break*?

BRIAN: Ninety percent of the calls are telemarketers trying to *talk* you *into* buying some obscure product.

KIM: Oh, I always *hang up* on them. It's my clients I'm complaining about.

Conversation Two:

MELISSA: I'm expecting John to *call* me *back*.

DANIEL: You'll have to wait a long time. He just *headed off for* Europe.

MELISSA: They have phones on the plane. He'll *get in touch*.

DANIEL: If I were he, I'd wait until I *got back* to call you.

Short Talk:

Cellular phones are extremely convenient, but being on a mobile phone creates a new set of problems. Often you experience static, although that's a *small price to pay* for the convenience of *being in touch* wherever you are—although many people do not see that as a positive thing. In the not-so-distant past, when you were on an airplane, you were incommunicado. Now, you *are* never *out of touch*, whether you're flying through the air or *walking down* the street. Another potential problem is getting *put on hold*. Often the person forgets about you, and you can *bank on* being disconnected.

Fill in the blanks to complete the sentences:

16. Thanks for calling. I'll _____ to you as soon as I can.

17. We _____ Fifth Avenue in the middle of a storm to watch the snow fall.

18. Ever since the news of my son's birth, the phone has been
    _____.

19. As soon as I _____ this report, I'll send it over to you.

20. I will definitely be on time; you can _____ it.

21. I had to _____ on the telemarketer because he wouldn't take "no" for an answer.

22. I tried to _____ with you while you were in Europe, but I couldn't reach you.

23. There is someone calling on the other line; I will have to _____ for a minute.

24. He would have _____ you _____ right away, but he couldn't find your phone number.

25. _____ you still _____ with that woman you used to live with in college?

26. Mr. Tisch _____ home as soon as he finished his dinner at the Chinese restaurant.

27. It's a shame that we've _____ all these years—I've missed you!

28. Working long hours is a _____ for having such a glamorous job.

29. I didn't want to go at first, but they _____ me _____ going with them.

30. _____! I can't finish all this work!

Answer Key

1. constantly ring
2. end a telephone call
3. return a call
4. depart for
5. make an effort to communicate with
6. make things easier for someone
7. return
8. make one caller wait while you talk to someone else or do another task
9. be in communication
10. not be in communication
11. stroll along
12. little cost for great benefit
13. complete
14. convince
15. depend on something happening with certainty

16. get back
17. walked down
18. ringing off the hook
19. finish up
20. bank on
21. hang up
22. get in touch
23. put you on hold
24. called (you) back
25. are (you still) in touch
26. headed off for
27. been out of touch
28. small price to pay
29. talked (me) into
30. give me a break

8 Relaxing

Match each word or phrase to its meaning:

1. sit around   unfold or unpack

2. skim through   lower oneself into

3. stretch out   relax, be lazy

4. spread out   read quickly to get the general gist

5. pick out   cause to leave; cast away; remove from

6. open up   casually glance through, as with a book or magazine

7. kick off   turn off

8. flop down   remove from (a list)

9. flip through   open and lay down, as on a table

10. switch off   lie down with the body extended

11. sit through   relax and get comfortable in a chair

12. cross off   let oneself fall or drop down loosely

13. sink into   be seated

14. sit back   remain seated throughout or for the duration of

15. laze around   select; choose

Can you figure out the meanings of the italicized words in the following passages?

Conversation One:

JASON: Let's *sit around* the table and *skim through* the paper to find out what's going on tonight.

MELANIE: I've already *spread* it *out*. Just *pick out* a section and *open* it *up*.

JASON: Great. But I think the cat's *stretched out* on the part I want to read. *Kick* him *off* the table, will you?

Conversation Two:

CATHY: I was so tired, I *flopped down* on the sofa the minute I got home.

JASON: You've been working much too hard. You have to learn to relax.

CATHY: That word's not in my vocabulary. I can't even *flip through* a magazine without thinking about work.

JASON: Try *sitting through* a two-day conference. That should dull your mind to work.

Short Talk:

At the end of the day, I always look in my date book and make sure I've *crossed off* everything I needed to do. Then I *kick off* my shoes, *sink into* an easy chair, and *sit back* and relax. I might *turn on* some music, but generally I prefer silence when I *laze around* the house. Most of my friends like listening to classical music, but *sitting through* a concert is my idea of torture. I prefer to *switch off* everything and sit in peace.

Fill in the blanks to complete the sentences:

16. We had to _____ a day-long lecture.

17. When I go on vacation, I _____ most of the day on the beach.

18. She was glad to _____ her high heeled shoes after the long day at the office.

19. We _____ in the classroom for hours waiting for the professor to arrive.

20. Let's _____ the blueprints on the long table over there.

21. I think I know how to fix the photocopy machine, but I'll _____ the instruction manual before I start just to make sure.

22. The board members _____ new furniture for the office.

23. After working in the field all day, I look forward to _____ with my newspaper.

24. They both like to _____ the comfortable sofa to watch the evening news.

25. I _____ on my towel on the beach and sunbathed all day.

26. Let's _____ the map and plot our vacation.

27. My son _____ on his bed after the long and tiring soccer game.

28. Don't forget to _____ the TV before you go to bed.

29. I think we should _____ the meeting with the tax collector _____ today's agenda.

30. The store owner _____ the catalog, but he couldn't make a decision on what to order.

Answer Key

1. be seated
2. read quickly to get the general gist
3. lie down with the body extended
4. open and lay down, as on a table
5. select; choose
6. unfold or unpack
7. cause to leave; cast away; remove from
8. let oneself fall or drop down loosely
9. casually glance through, as with a book or magazine
10. turn off
11. remain seated throughout or for the duration of
12. remove from (a list)
13. lower oneself into
14. relax and get comfortable in a chair
15. relax, be lazy
16. sit through
17. laze around
18. kick off
19. sat around
20. spread out
21. skim through
22. picked out
23. sitting back
24. sink into
25. stretched out
26. open up
27. flopped down
28. switch off
29. cross (the meeting with the tax collector) off
30. flipped through

9 Eating

Match each word or phrase to its meaning:

1. move away — consume food undisturbed
2. sweep up — slice into pieces
3. boss around — escape from
4. eat in peace — collect and remove
5. clean up — eat all of
6. relax over — eat a great deal
7. cut up — not be so strict or demanding with
8. put away — consume all of
9. pig out — put things back in order
10. set out — maintain at a lower level
11. cut (a person) slack — distance or remove oneself from
12. get out of — arrange or display
13. polish off — return something to where it is normally stored
14. finish off — take a rest while doing something
15. keep down — haughtily command someone to do things

Can you figure out the meanings of the italicized words in the following passages?

Conversation One:

MIKE: *Move away* from the table, would you? I need to *sweep up* those crumbs you're dropping.

BRENDA: Stop *bossing* me *around*. Why don't you let me *eat in peace* and *clean up* later?

MIKE: While you're *relaxing over* your lunch, I've got to *cut up* the vegetables for tonight's soup, wash and *put away* the dishes, iron and *spread out* the tablecloth, and polish and *set out* the silver. Now would you *cut me some slack* and *get out of* my way?

Conversation Two:

BRENDA: You sure *polished off* that cake.

JENNIFER: If there had been another one, I would have *finished off* that one too.

BRENDA: How do you *keep* your weight *down* when you are constantly *pigging out*?

JENNIFER: I *get out of* the house and exercise regularly, so I never put on any weight.

Short Talk:

Are we what we eat? We want to eat low-fat, low-salt diets in smoke-free environments—at least when others are watching. Left alone, we *pig out, finishing off* the chocolate cake all by ourselves. We can laugh at our own foibles, but we won't *cut* anyone else any *slack* and let them eat in peace. Our policy seems to be, let us eat cake and let everyone else eat whole wheat bread, or else.

Fill in the blanks to complete the sentences:

16. I feel sick after _____ on that giant tub of ice cream.

17. Let's sit down and _____ a hot cup of tea.

18. The former chief of staff never _____ people _____. He was always polite and courteous.

19. He _____ the entire box of chocolates himself in under five minutes.

20. He _____ from the dog when it started to growl at him.

21. Please _____ your voices _____ while we are filming.

22. When I was late for the fifth day in a row, my teacher told me that he couldn't _____ me any _____ this time and I'd have to report to the principal.

23. Every winter we _____ all the outdoor furniture.

24. Who's going to stay and _____ after the party?

25. John agreed to _____ the sawdust when we finish sawing.

26. My assistant will show you how the photographs should be _____ on the page.

27. I think we should _____ the cake _____ into smaller pieces, as more guests than expected are coming.

28. The workers _____ the beef stew in no time.

29. Let's _____ and talk business later.

30. He barely _____ the path of the train.

Answer Key

1. distance or remove oneself from
2. collect and remove
3. haughtily command someone to do things
4. consume food undisturbed
5. put things back in order
6. take a rest while doing something
7. slice into pieces
8. return something to where it is normally stored
9. eat a great deal
10. arrange or display
11. not be so strict or demanding with
12. escape from
13. eat all of
14. consume all of
15. maintain at a lower level

16. pigging out
17. relax over
18. bossed (people) around
19. finished off
20. moved away
21. keep (your voices) down
22. cut (me any) slack
23. put away
24. clean up
25. sweep up
26. set out
27. cut (the cake) up
28. polished off
29. eat in peace
30. got out of

10 Relationships

Match each word or phrase to its meaning:

1.	touch on	assemble one's things to leave
2.	stand up for	show excessive concern
3.	believe in	give up (an opportunity)
4.	split up	have faith in
5.	take after	get in the way of
6.	wind up	tolerate, put up with
7.	pack up	support
8.	pick up	meet and get together with someone to whom you are attracted
9.	bottle up	finish up, end up
10.	fuss over	think of
11.	interfere with	break up; end a relationship
12.	pass up	mention
13.	come up with	surrender
14.	stand for	have similar characteristics
15.	give in	keep within oneself

Can you figure out the meanings of the italicized words in the following passages?

Conversation One:

ALEX: The speaker *touched on* a sensitive subject.

SHARON: You mean the one about people who don't *stand up for* what they *believe in*?

ALEX: No, the part about couples who *split up* because they no longer are sensitive to one another's feelings.

Conversation Two:

KELLY: You really *take after* your mother.

RODNEY: I take that as a compliment.

KELLY: It was meant as a criticism. You've really inherited all of her worst habits.

RODNEY: I suppose you'd like me to *pack up* and move back to my mother's so you can go out and *pick up* some stud in a bar!

Short Talk:

I like people that don't *bottle up* their feelings. I also like people who *fuss over* me; people who agree with me; and people who don't *interfere with* my way of doing things. I may be a little selfish, and I rarely *give in* to other people's demands, but at least I know what I want. I *passed up* the chance to marry a really, rich, intelligent person because he never *came up* with any plans that remotely amused me. In fact, I've decided that I won't *stand for* another boring night. I may *finish up* alone in this world, but however I *wind up*, I'll have done it my way.

Fill in the blanks to complete the sentences:

16. Your new baby certainly doesn't _____ you; she looks more like her mother.

17. Unless you _____ a better idea, I plan to watch TV all night.

18. It is dangerous to _____ strange men on the street, because you never can tell just what kind of people they are.

19. The speaker _____ the causes of divorce, but did not go into detail.

20. If you don't _____ yourself, it is difficult to trust anyone else.

21. You might want to _____ from time to time; it's not good to be so stubborn.

22. After the game, we all _____ in my kitchen and had pizza.

23. It's often healthier to express your emotions rather than to _____ them _____.

24. If the Jacksons _____, how will they divide their property?

25. If you can't _____ what you believe in, you might as well never open your mouth.

26. Do not _____ the movements of the emergency crew.

27. When I quit my job, I _____ my belongings and left by the side door.

28. Never _____ an opportunity to go to a fancy party.

29. My mother still _____ me, and I love it.

30. I find it difficult to _____ insulting behavior.

Answer Key

1. mention
2. support
3. have faith in
4. break up; end a relationship
5. have similar characteristics
6. finish up, end up
7. assemble one's things to leave
8. meet and get together with someone to whom you are attracted
9. keep within oneself
10. show excessive concern
11. get in the way of
12. give up an opportunity
13. think of
14. tolerate, put up with
15. surrender
16. take after
17. come up with
18. pick up
19. touched on
20. believe in
21. give in
22. wound up
23. bottle (them) up
24. split up
25. stand up for
26. interfere with
27. packed up
28. pass up
29. fusses over
30. stand for

11 Visiting

Match the word or phrase to its meaning:

1. stop by — leave
2. drop off — visit a person or place briefly while on the way to somewhere else
3. hold off — complete; bring to an end
4. get away — visit or go to some place
5. drop by — begin or venture forth
6. set off — accompany someone to his departure
7. pass by — go or leave some place
8. start out — handle; take control of
9. check on — resolve a problem
10. put out a fire — occur unexpectedly
11. plan ahead — leave something
12. wrap up — look at or take care of
13. see off — arrange beforehand in order to be prepared
14. crop up — visit someone
15. deal with — wait or refrain from doing something

Can you figure out the meanings of the italicized words in the following passages?

Conversation One:

AARON: I'll *stop by* after work and *drop off* that book I borrowed. Then we can go to the movies.

NATALIE: *Hold off* until 7:30, since I won't be able to *get away* until the kids have eaten dinner.

AARON: I'll *drop by* at 6 and we'll *set off* when you're ready.

Conversation Two:

TIFFANY: I haven't heard from Peter; he said he'd *pass by* here before *starting out* on his camping trip.

NATALIE: He had to *check on* a few things at the office before he left.

TIFFANY: A few *fires to put out*, no doubt.

NATALIE: He *plans ahead*, so I'm sure there was nothing unexpected to *wrap up*.

Short Talk:

When you *see* a visitor *off* at the airport, it is important to arrive in plenty of time so that the passenger is not nervous that she will miss her flight. Problems like road closures or heavy traffic may *crop up*, so you want to be prepared to *deal with* unexpected emergencies. If you *drop off* your friend early, she'll be able to sit back and relax at the gate.

Fill in the blanks to complete the sentences:

16. Let's _____ the meeting _____ by having everyone introduce themselves.

17. My wife and I will wait with you until the train comes and then _____ you _____ at the train station.

18. If we have time, I'd like to _____ the pharmacy before we go to the restaurant.

19. I'm glad we have such a reliable babysitter because now I don't feel like I have to call and _____ the kids.

20. My chauffeur will _____ your tuxedo at the office at 6 P.M. so you can dress for dinner.

21. The new personnel office is _____ employee complaints swiftly and effectively.

22. Until we actually have the money set aside for it, I'd like to _____ on purchasing a new air conditioner.

23. The boss hoped that by talking to the angry employee he could _____ before it started.

24. A good financial manager will always set money aside for unexpected expenses that _____.

25. I'll _____ the embassy at 2 P.M. to apply for another visa.

26. She wants to _____ the library after class to return a few books.

27. If we _____ with our finances, we shouldn't have any trouble keeping to our budget.

28. If we work quickly, we'll be able to _____ for a few minutes to have lunch.

29. They _____ early in the morning so they could reach Manhattan by nightfall.

30. I hope to _____ this project by June.

Answer Key

1. visit or go to some place
2. leave something
3. wait or refrain from doing something
4. leave
5. visit someone
6. go or leave some place
7. visit a person or place briefly while on the way to somewhere else
8. begin or venture forth
9. look at or take care of
10. handle; resolve
11. arrange beforehand in order to be prepared
12. complete; bring to an end
13. accompany someone to his departure
14. occur unexpectedly
15. handle; take control of
16. start (the meeting) out
17. see (you) off
18. stop by
19. check on
20. drop off
21. dealing with
22. hold off
23. put out the fire
24. crop up
25. drop by
26. pass by
27. plan ahead
28. get away
29. set off
30. wrap up

12 | Alternative Plans

Match each word or phrase to its meaning:

1.	carry on	supply information about
2.	take over	take into consideration
3.	fill in	continue on too long
4.	go through	to take something too seriously, to panic
5.	check off	to stop functioning, fall to pieces
6.	lose one's cool	continue doing
7.	feel up to	make; file for
8.	put in	execute; use
9.	account for	pull into a bad mood
10.	come apart	make a note of; make a mark next to
11.	call for	stop something before it grows too large
12.	drag on	require; need
13.	nip something in the bud	assume the responsibility for and execution of
14.	bring in	be ready and able to do something
15.	drag down	read or look at

Can you figure out the meanings of the italicized words in the following passages?

Conversation One:

POLLY: Delilah quit, but we'll just have to *carry on* without her. You can *take over* her job.

MATILDA: OK. Just *fill* me *in* on what I need to do.

POLLY: First, you should *go through* this manual and *check off* the tasks that you need help with.

Conversation Two:

POLLY: Hey, don't *lose your cool*. I know you can do it.

MATILDA: I just don't *feel up to* doing all of this by myself.

POLLY: Don't *give in* before you've started.

MATILDA: I'm not. I just think I need to *put in* a request for some help, that's all.

Short Talk:

All operational plans must *account for* potential problems. If one plan *comes apart*, you may have to try an alternative plan. Successful handling of problems *calls for* strategic planning. Rather than letting a problem *drag on*, *nip it in the bud* immediately and *bring in* your contingency plan. Be on top of the situation, and don't let it *drag you down*.

Fill in the blanks to complete the sentences:

16. Don't let his moody disposition _____ you _____ while you're working.

17. We weren't able to _____ with our work when the storm knocked the electricity out.

18. He _____ his own favorite employees when he saw how poorly things were being run.

19. _____ me _____ on the progress down at the construction site—I don't know what's going on.

20. The high incidence of theft in the office _____ an immediate investigation.

21. When you _____ it, let's take a walk down by the beach.

22. No one was available to _____ her job, as she was transferred quite suddenly.

23. Go through this list of items and _____ what you think you'll need.

24. I _____ for a leave of absence at work, but I'm afraid it may not get approved.

25. At first there seemed to be a conflict between the two sides, but we quickly _____.

26. You'll have to _____ the fact that many employees will get angry if you set the deadline.

27. I'm glad you didn't _____ when they asked you all those questions in the job interview.

28. Her plan _____ because she had not researched it thoroughly.

29. His speech _____ for hours, boring the audience to tears.

30. I _____ the article and found two errors.

Answer Key

1. continue doing
2. assume the responsibility for and execution of
3. supply information about
4. read or look at
5. make a note of; make a mark next to
6. to take something too seriously, panic
7. be ready and able to do something
8. make; file for
9. take into consideration
10. to stop functioning, fall to pieces
11. require; need
12. continue on too long
13. stop something before it grows too large
14. execute; use
15. pull into a bad mood
16. drag (you) down
17. carry on
18. brought in
19. fill (me) in
20. calls for
21. feel up to it
22. take over
23. check off
24. put in
25. nipped it in the bud
26. account for
27. lose your cool
28. came apart
29. dragged on
30. went through

13 Establishing Rapport

Match each word or phrase to its meaning:

1. hit it off	insult; embarrass	
2. let down	extend an invitation to one's home	
3. protect from	condone; like	
4. hold against	disappoint	
5. hold up	avoid	
6. lay off	date	
7. put off	stop; leave alone	
8. put down	think less of someone because of something	
9. steer clear of	work out to be	
10. tick off	excite, start up	
11. go out	annoy	
12. invite over	guard against	
13. approve of	keep up	
14. stir up	offend, disgust	
15. turn out	establish rapport; like someone immediately	

Can you figure out the meanings of the italicized words in the following passages?

Conversation One:

SYDNEY: Finally, I *went out* with a guy I can trust. I can't believe how well we *hit it off*. He *invited* me *over* again tonight.

PAT: Be careful. You know I don't *approve of* quick romances. He might *let* you *down*.

SYDNEY: You're just trying to *protect* me *from* being hurt. I'm sure it will *turn out* okay.

Conversation Two:

JAKE: If I told you I thought you had a beautiful body, would you *hold* it *against* me?

JULIA: Ha ha, very funny. Would you *lay off*? I'm simply trying to *hold up* my end of a pleasant conversation, but you keep making insinuating remarks.

JAKE: I'm sorry—the last thing I want to do is to *tick* you *off* and *stir up* trouble between us. From now on, I promise that even your mother would *approve of* the comments I make.

Short Talk:

Someone who is too truthful can *put* people *off*. Most people prefer white lies. They don't want to be *put down* in front of others. Friends don't want to be criticized by friends; it reminds them of their teachers or, worse, their parents. You should *steer clear of* commenting on another's eccentricities unless these eccentricities really *tick* you *off*. You don't want to *stir up* trouble, especially with your friends.

Fill in the blanks to complete the sentences:

16. If you continue to _____ people _____, you'll find yourself without friends.

17. My daughter wanted to _____ with the boy next door, but she's too young to go on a date.

18. The two new managers _____ well the first time they met.

19. I thought only ten or 15 people would come, but as it _____, we had over 50.

20. You can't count on him doing the job right; he'll _____ you _____.

21. I've _____ my end of the bargain, but you haven't done anything that we agreed to do.

22. His constant complaining really _____ me _____.

23. My younger sister is always trying to _____ trouble in the family.

24. The security guards will _____ you _____ the rioters.

25. I _____ him _____ for coffee after the movie, but he had to be home by eleven.

26. Your past actions may be _____ you even if you apologize.

27. Her perfume was too strong—it really _____ me _____.

28. Try to _____ parties while you're studying for your exams.

29. I asked him to _____, but he just kept teasing me.

30. She didn't _____ her son's new girlfriend.

Answer Key

1. establish rapport; like someone immediately
2. disappoint
3. guard against
4. think less of someone because of something
5. keep up
6. stop; leave alone
7. offend, disgust
8. insult; embarrass
9. avoid
10. annoy
11. date
12. extend an invitation to one's home
13. condone; like
14. excite, start up
15. work out to be
16. put (people) down
17. go out
18. hit it off
19. turned out
20. let (you) down
21. held up
22. ticks (me) off
23. stir up
24. protect (you) from
25. invited (him) over
26. held against
27. put (me) off
28. steer clear of
29. lay off
30. approve of

14 Quitting

Match each word or phrase to its meaning:

1. resign from   consider

2. run away from   give some consideration to

3. think over   begin

4. think through   allow someone else to have

5. get going   assume the responsibility for

6. rule out   avoid or walk away from

7. kick out   observe a situation

8. start up   fire someone; stop employment

9. have to   exclude

10. fill in for   consider all aspects of something; look at all the facts

11. look around   must

12. take on   no longer work with or for

13. think about   to reach a favorable agreement on the terms of a business transaction

14. give up   replace; substitute

15. bargain for   get started, act

Can you figure out the meanings of the italicized words in the following passages?

Conversation One:

BRENT: I'm sorry to say that I'm *resigning from* my job today.

MAUREEN: You can't *run away* from responsibility. *Think it over* and give me your decision tomorrow.

BRENT: No, I've *thought* it *through* very carefully, and I've decided that now is the time for me to *get going* with my career.

Conversation Two:

JACKIE: I haven't *ruled out* the possibility of quitting.

GILLIAN: They won't *kick* you *out,* so if you want to *start up* your own company, you'll *have to* quit.

JACKIE: Who would they get to *fill in for* me, I wonder?

GILLIAN: *Look around.* No one here could take on your job.

Short Talk:

Are you *thinking about giving up* your job? It is best to not *resign from* the job you have if you do not have another one waiting for you. You are in a much stronger position to *bargain for* a better salary and benefits if you are not *depending on* the income from your new job to pay your rent. Furthermore, the longer you are on the job market without a job, the less appealing you may seem to a potential employer. If no one else wants to hire you, why should she or he take the chance? *Think through* your situation before you act.

Fill in the blanks to complete the sentences:

16. He was hired because he proved in his last job that he doesn't _____ responsibility.

17. We need to _____ with that project if we hope to finish it by the end of the week.

18. Her dream was to _____ her own veterinary practice.

19. She stopped and _____ and realized she was lost.

20. If you have a goal, don't ever _____ on trying to reach it.

21. Lately I've been _____ adding a second floor to my house.

22. The lieutenant _____ his post in light of the allegation against him.

23. We still can't _____ arson as a possible cause of the fire.

24. According to the law, all citizens _____ pay taxes.

25. My many years of experience allowed me to _____ a better salary.

26. I didn't really want to, but I finally agreed to _____ her projects so that we could finish the job on time.

27. She came in on her day off to _____ Heidi, who was sick.

28. He was _____ of the department because his work was consistently poorly done.

29. You should _____ this _____ before resigning, because there's no turning back.

30. After _____ it _____, I have decided to keep my money in a savings account rather than in mutual funds.

Answer Key

1. no longer work with or for
2. avoid or walk away from
3. give some consideration to
4. consider all aspects of something; look at all the facts
5. get started, act
6. exclude
7. fire someone; stop employment
8. begin
9. must
10. replace; substitute
11. observe a situation
12. assume the responsibility for
13. consider
14. allow someone else to have
15. to reach a favorable agreement on the terms of a business transaction

16. run away from
17. get going
18. start up
19. looked around
20. give up
21. thinking about
22. resigned from
23. rule out
24. have to
25. bargain for
26. take on
27. fill in for
28. kicked out
29. think (this) through
30. thinking (it) over

15 Working Together

Match the word or phrase to its meaning:

1.	loosen up	support
2.	take to heart	avoid
3.	strike out	cooperate with
4.	keep away	appear; arrive
5.	fall over	inquire about with various people
6.	ask around	consider seriously, be affected by
7.	check up on	accomplish tasks together with others
8.	confide in	share one's thoughts with someone
9.	bring up to date	strive to attain a goal
10.	work together	go ahead with something new
11.	be there for	separate from
12.	go along with	provide the most recent information available
13.	break away	relax
14.	show up	investigate
15.	work towards	collapse

Can you figure out the meanings of the italicized words in the following passages?

Conversation One:

HENRY: *Loosen up*, will you? Don't *take* this *to heart* so much.

LIZA: I have to do more than just *show up* for work.

HENRY: I know, but you're going to *fall over* from exhaustion one of these days.

Conversation Two:

LIZA: Why don't you *ask around* about Bob and see what kind of a worker he is?

HENRY: I've already *checked up on* him, but I don't want to say anything right away.

LIZA: You can *confide in* me. What's the story?

HENRY: I'll *bring* you *up to date* at the staff meeting. All I can tell you now is, *keep away* from him as much as possible.

Short Talk:

When you *work together* in a group, it is important to *be there for* your colleagues. You may not agree with everything they say, but, in the end, you should *go along with* the group consensus. If you *break away* from the group, your day-to-day relationship with your colleagues will suffer. Try to work with the group and *work towards* a harmonious consensus. *Striking out* on your own may cause problems with your peers.

Fill in the blanks to complete the sentences:

16. _____ from the fire! It's dangerous!

17. She wanted to _____ his qualifications again before hiring him.

18. It is painful to _____ from a tightly knit group.

19. Our management is _____ a perfect safety record at the construction site.

20. It's all right to _____ the group as long as you think what the group is doing is right.

21. If I could just learn to _____, I know I would sleep better at night.

22. Mr. Buchs _____ from heat exhaustion when the air conditioning went off.

23. The union chief was leery of _____ me because I was in management.

24. Even though I _____ late every morning, I always finish my work on time.

25. If both of our teams _____, we'll probably make the deadline.

26. George _____ his sister when she had that accident; he even had to miss a week of work.

27. She _____ your advice _____ and hired two more employees.

28. Let's _____ the office to see if anyone knows a good restaurant near here.

29. The secretary will _____ you _____ on what was decided at the meeting.

30. When Tim realized he didn't want to work for his father, he decided to _____ on his own.

Answer Key

1. relax
2. consider seriously, be affected by
3. go ahead with something new
4. avoid
5. collapse
6. inquire about with various people
7. investigate
8. share one's thoughts with someone
9. provide the latest information available
10. accomplish tasks together with others
11. support
12. cooperate with
13. separate from
14. appear; arrive
15. strive to attain a goal
16. keep away
17. check up on
18. break away
19. working towards
20. go along with
21. loosen up
22. fell over
23. confiding in
24. show up
25. work together
26. was there for
27. took (your advice) to heart
28. ask around
29. bring (you) up to date
30. strike out

16 Clothes Shopping

Match each word or phrase to its meaning:

1. do up   raise; lift up

2. lace up   put clothes on to see how they look and fit

3. put on   curl or fold upward

4. fasten up   sell, expecting to get a percentage of the sale as compensation

5. pull up   fasten as with string, etcetera

6. roll up   to make smaller in choice or width

7. hang on   approach; come up to

8. mark up   place (clothes) on the body

9. try on   indicate, as with chalk

10. give up   put fancy or formal clothes on

11. narrow down   fasten

12. work on commission   test something to see if it appeals

13. descend on   stop what one is saying or doing

14. try out   quit, stop trying

15. dress up   secure, as with buttons, etcetera

Can you figure out the meanings of the italicized words in the following passages?

Conversation One:

DONALD: Can you *do* me *up*? I can't fasten these buttons.

JILL: OK, I'll help you with the buttons, but you have to *lace up* your own shoes, and *put on* your own pants.

DONALD: I just asked you to *fasten* me *up*, not to dress me completely.

Conversation Two:

LORNA: Either *pull up* your pants or *roll up* the cuffs. They're dragging across the floor.

TREVOR: *Hang on.* I'm going to have them altered. The tailor will *mark* them *up* and fix the length.

LORNA: You should have *tried on* the gray pair of trousers; they would have fit you better than the blue ones or those green ones.

TREVOR: I *give up.* I *narrowed down* the selection to these two pairs, and now you want me to try the gray pair.

Short Talk:

When you enter a clothing store, you can tell if the staff *works on commission* or receives a flat salary. The commissioned staff *descends on* you like vultures and will insist that you *try out* everything in the store. If you *dress up* when you go to these fancy boutiques, the staff will think that you are a serious customer. On the other hand, you can pretend to be above it all and wear informal clothes.

Fill in the blanks to the complete sentences:

16. I only like to _____ on the weekends when I go out to dinner.

17. The foreman _____ the walls, indicating where the carpenters were to make the changes.

18. I can _____ you _____ as soon as I finish dressing myself.

19. Here. _____ this jacket _____.

20. We _____ on trying to find a tie that matched his bright orange and green suit.

21. Lisa has needed help _____ her shoes ever since she hurt her back skiing.

22. Now _____ a minute! You have no right talking to me like that.

23. The crowds _____ the new president, trying to shake his hand.

24. You'll have to _____ it _____ to see if it fits in the waist.

25. He _____ his sleeves because it was getting so hot.

26. If you're not sure about buying this new car, ask if you can _____ it _____ for a week first.

27. Most clothes salesmen _____ to try to earn more money.

28. Firemen have to _____ their gear completely before entering a fire.

29. After two hours, we were able to _____ the choices for chairman to Mr. Jones and Mr. Byles.

30. _____ your trousers! They're falling down.

Answer Key

1. fasten

2. fasten as with string, etcetera

3. place (clothes) on the body

4. secure, as with buttons, etcetera

5. raise; lift up

6. curl or fold upward

7. stop what one is saying or doing

8. indicate, as with chalk

9. put clothes on to see how they look and fit

10. quit, stop trying

11. to make smaller in choice or width

12. to sell expecting to get a percentage of the sale as compensation

13. approach; come up to

14. test something to see if it appeals to one

15. put fancy or formal clothes on

16. dress up

17. marked up

18. do (you) up

19. try (this jacket) on

20. gave up

21. lacing up

22. hang on

23. descended on

24. put (it) on

25. rolled up

26. try (it) out

27. work on commission

28. fasten up

29. narrow down

30. pull up

17 Moving Furniture

Match each word or phrase to its meaning:

1. rub off   stay in some place with an expectation of some kind

2. wipe off   wait somewhere

3. scrub off   distribute or allot

4. divide up   raise; pick up

5. set aside   place on the floor

6. wait for   be visible

7. move into   remove or take off by friction

8. wait around   package; put into boxes

9. show up   notice; remember

10. pack up   remain inactive until some specific thing occurs

11. leave for   place inside of

12. hang around   take off with a cloth

13. set down   to place apart

14. lift up   put off until; not do until

15. take note of   to remove by rubbing vigorously, as with a brush

Success with American Idioms

Can you figure out the meanings of the italicized words in the following passages?

Conversation One:

MANUEL: Ugh! The grease on this counter *rubbed off* on my hand.

SELENA: *Wipe* it *off* with this towel, and be careful how you handle things. We don't want that to *show up* on the upholstery later.

MANUEL: I'll get some soap and *scrub* it *off*.

Conversation Two:

SELENA: Let's *divide up* the chores. Why don't you *set* all the heavy furniture *aside* and *wait for* Mark to come and help us *move* it *into* the truck?

MANUEL: I don't want to *wait around* all day for him to *show up*.

SELENA: Calm down. We could *pack up* the china until he gets here.

MANUEL: Let's *leave* it *for* tomorrow. I just don't want to *hang around* all day in this hot apartment.

Short Talk:

When you move antique furniture, it is important to treat it gently. You cannot *set* quality furniture *down* carelessly because the sudden movement might weaken its legs. When you *lift up* a chair, you should hold on to the seat, not the back. When you move a dresser, you should *take out* all the drawers. When you move a table, you should maintain a firm grip on it. If you *take note of* this advice, your antique furniture should last for hundreds of years.

Fill in the blanks to complete the sentences:

16. I'll _____ you at the airport in the main lobby.

17. We should _____ the books in smaller boxes so they aren't so heavy.

18. It's always boring when you have to _____ a train station when a train is late.

19. Let's _____ this farm equipment _____ the barn before the storm strikes.

20. I've been trying to _____ the dirty spot _____ the wall but it won't come off.

21. The boys had to _____ the graffiti _____ the walls of the building.

22. We _____ three computers for the temporary help this weekend.

23. She _____ the fact that the clerk undercharged her for the armchair, but she didn't say anything.

24. Please _____ this chair _____ carefully.

25. Victoria was enraged when stains _____ on her priceless sofa the day she moved in.

26. The waitress _____ the counter before she took our order.

27. It was crucial to the family morale that the inheritance be _____ evenly.

28. They _____ for two hours, but the bus never came.

29. Let's _____ this _____ another day when we have more staff on hand.

30. I wasn't able to _____ the garage door because the lock was jammed.

Answer Key

1. remove or take off by friction
2. take off with a cloth
3. to remove by rubbing vigorously, as with a brush
4. to distribute or allot
5. to place apart
6. to remain inactive until some specific thing occurs
7. place inside of
8. stay in some place with an expectation of some kind
9. appear; arrive
10. package; put into boxes
11. put off until; not do until
12. wait somewhere
13. place on the floor
14. raise; pick up
15. notice; remember

16. wait for
17. pack up
18. hang around
19. move (this farm equipment) into
20. rub (the dirty spot) off
21. scrub (the graffiti) off
22. set aside
23. took note of
24. set (this chair) down
25. showed up
26. wiped off
27. divided up
28. waited around
29. leave (this) for
30. lift up

Match each word or phrase to its meaning:

1. think of   take care of; be concerned about

2. hope for   have the minimum of what is wanted or needed

3. hole up   to go from childhood to adulthood

4. come along   anticipate

5. lock out of   look for; want

6. look out for   secure the doors so that one can't get back in

7. close up   be discovered; show up

8. turn up   feel about; have an opinion about

9. settle on   count on; expect to

10. shop around for   renovate; repair

11. be enough for   stay in some place and not leave

12. grow up   repeat, go over

13. figure on   decide on; make a decision about

14. run through   lock doors and set alarms

15. fix up   show up; appear

Can you figure out the meanings of the italicized words in the following passages?

Conversation One:

BOB: What do you *think of* this apartment?

ASHLEY: It's much less than I *hoped for*, but perhaps I can *fix it up* a little.

BOB: You can always *hole up* here until something better *comes along*.

Conversation Two:

MARILYN: Oh, no! I think I've *locked* us *out* of the apartment. I can't find the keys anywhere.

STAN: Look down. You dropped them on the mat.

MARILYN: Thank goodness you're *looking out for* me.

STAN: I watched you *close up* the building, so I knew the keys would *turn up* somewhere around here.

Short Talk:

Before you *settle on* an apartment, you should *shop around for* different options. First, consider location. Is it close to schools, shops, transportation? Second, consider size. Is it large enough? Will there *be enough* room *for* your children to *grow up* in? Finally, consider price. Is it within your budget? (You should *figure on* spending more than you intended). You should not make the decision alone; *run through* all the pros and cons carefully with your family and your real estate agent.

Fill in the blanks to complete the sentences:

16. The factory _____ when it went bankrupt.

17. We _____ ourselves _____ of the car, and now we're stuck here at the gas station.

18. No one will _____ less _____ you as long as you keep trying.

19. Since the house required extensive repairs, we didn't think we could _____ it _____ ourselves.

20. Ms. Pitkin _____ a better deal on a used car.

21. I'd like to _____ these figures one more time before we decide to make the purchase.

22. I rest easy knowing that my staff is _____ my business.

23. She had _____ a much more favorable review by the book critic.

24. Should an engineering job _____, I'll be the first to let you know.

25. One can always _____ people spending what they expect to earn.

26. When that missing file _____, I would appreciate it if you would call me.

27. We need to make sure there _____ textbooks _____ everyone in the class.

28. We weren't able to _____ an investment strategy that meets all our needs.

29. I wish the children in this country could _____ with fewer negative influences.

30. Every time Ted has a fight with his wife, he _____ in his office and won't go home.

Answer Key

1. feel about; have an opinion about

2. anticipate

3. stay in some place and not leave

4. show up; appear

5. secure the doors so that one can't get back in

6. take care of; be concerned about

7. lock doors and set alarms

8. be discovered; show up

9. decide on; make a decision about

10. look for, want

11. to have the minimum of what is wanted or needed

12. to go from childhood to adulthood

13. count on; expect to

14. repeat, go over

15. renovate; repair

16. closed up

17. locked (ourselves) out

18. think (less) of

19. fix (it) up

20. shopped around for

21. run through

22. looking out for

23. hoped for

24. come along

25. figure on

26. turns up

27. are enough (textbooks) for

28. settle on

29. grow up

30. holes up

19 Planning a Project

Match each word or phrase to its meaning:

1. tie up   fit in; make room or time for

2. put off   let go of; cease to employ

3. stick with   not be able to accomplish because of lack of time

4. pull in   give to others to do

5. squeeze in   convince; win someone's agreement or understanding

6. muddle through   arrange for; bring in

7. lay off   bring in

8. impress upon   postpone

9. hold on to   redo; carry out again

10. look up   complete a large number of tasks rapidly

11. run out of time   figure out a way to do

12. farm out   occupy with something

13. churn out   search for information about

14. do over   not let go of; keep

15. call in   not give up on

Can you figure out the meanings of the italicized words in the following passages?

Conversation One:

COLIN: I'm all *tied up* on this one project; I'm going to have to *put* this other one *off* until next month.

PENNY: You *stick with* what you're doing. I'll *pull in* someone to help you.

COLIN: I don't need help with this project. I just can't *squeeze in* another.

Conversation Two:

PENNY: We'll just have to *muddle through*, I guess, until we get some help.

COLIN: We shouldn't have *laid off* the entire design department. We should have *impressed upon* management that we would be understaffed in an emergency.

PENNY: That's for sure. We should have *held on to* what we had.

COLIN: I guess we'd better *look up* some temp agencies and *call in* some temporary help. We need it.

Short Talk:

Often when there is too much work to do in a company or when employees *run out of time*, work is *farmed out* to people outside the company. These freelance workers can *churn out* work very quickly and, usually, less expensively than company employees can. Unfortunately, they do not always do it as well, and the employees sometimes have to *do* it *over*.

Fill in the blanks to complete the sentences:

16. _____ it; you'll reach your goal.

17. I'd rather give the work to our own employees than _____ it _____.

18. The firm _____ a consultant to work on the project.

19. The architect was all _____ with the skyscraper he was building, and couldn't take on any other projects.

20. If we had _____ our desperate financial situation _____ him, I think he would have approved the loan.

21. We lost the bonus because we _____, and didn't manage to finish the job by Friday.

22. Because of all the mistakes, I'll have to ask you to _____ this report _____.

23. If I can't _____ another doctor for your night shift, you'll have to stay.

24. Mark is a hard-working employee whom you'll want to _____.

25. We can't _____ this discussion _____ any longer. I need to talk to you right now.

26. I know you're busy, but if you can just _____ me _____, you won't regret it.

27. We_____ his number in the phone book.

28. This factory can _____ more shoes than any other factory on the East Coast.

29. We had to _____ a dozen employees due to slow sales.

30. He always finds a way to _____ every business crisis.

Answer Key

1. occupy with something
2. postpone
3. not give up on
4. arrange for; bring in
5. fit in; make room or time for
6. figure out a way to do
7. let go of; cease to employ
8. convince; win someone's agreement or understanding
9. not let go of; keep
10. search for information about
11. not be able to accomplish because of lack of time
12. give to others to do
13. complete a large number of tasks rapidly
14. redo; carry out again
15. bring in

16. stick with
17. farm (it) out
18. called in
19. tied up
20. impressed (our dire financial straits) upon
21. ran out of time
22. do (this report) over
23. pull in
24. hold on to
25. put (this discussion) off
26. squeeze (me) in
27. looked up
28. churn out
29. lay off
30. muddle through

20 Leaving the Office

Match each word or phrase to its meaning:

1. clean off   remove any unnecessary or inappropriate items from; put in order

2. take off   indicate that one is leaving by signing one's name

3. clean out   put in order

4. tidy up   cause not to operate or function

5. pull down   tell someone to leave

6. mill around   remove all unnecessary items from; put in order

7. pass on   slow down, bring to an end

8. send someone packing   make a place secure by locking doors and setting alarms

9. wind down   move around in a disorderly way

10. make off with   leave someone alone, stop nagging someone

11. sign in   give to others

12. sign out   steal something

13. get off someone's back   leave an area

14. shut off   lower something fastened from above

15. lock up   register; indicate one's presence

Can you figure out the meanings of the italicized words in the following passages?

Conversation One:

CLYDE: You should really *clean off* your desk before you *take off* each night. We need to *tidy up* the areas that a visitor might see. And if I were you, I'd *clean out* my desk while I was at it.

TINA: Thanks for the tip.

Conversation Two:

TINA: That Clyde is always ordering me around. He's not my boss! I wish he'd *get off my back*!

FRANCES: He is demanding, isn't he? Yesterday he told me to *pull down* the blinds and *lock up* my file drawers when I went out to lunch!

TINA: Does he think some stranger is going to walk by and *make off with* your computer during lunch?

FRANCES: Who knows? He even called the police about suspicious characters who were *milling around* the office recently. He wanted to *send* these innocent strangers *packing*!

Short Talk:

In some work places, guests are required to *sign in* at the reception area when they enter the building, and to *sign out* when they leave. These security measures are necessary to make sure that company secrets are not *passed on* to outsiders. When work is *winding down* for the day, security personnel check that all visitors have left the building. Then they *shut off* the lights and *lock up* the building.

Fill in the blanks to complete the sentences:

16. Ellen wanted her boss to _____ ;
    she was tired of hearing his complaints.

17. Things at the office always _____
    early on the day before a holiday.

18. We _____ the basement and
    found all kinds of memorabilia.

19. According to our records, Mr. Smith _____
    of the hotel early this morning.

20. During the burglary, the thief _____
    my stereo.

21. Let's _____ everything _____ the shelves
    and arrange all the books in alphabetical order.

22. Once I _____ this building ____, no one can enter
    it without triggering the alarm.

23. Please _____ at the secretary's
    desk in the lower lobby.

24. Thomas _____ every night at 6
    o'clock and goes straight home.

25. He _____ the good news to his wife.

26. The huge crowd _____ the theater,
    waiting for the doors to open.

27. _____ the shades! It's too sunny.

28. Don't forget to _____ the air
    conditioner when you leave the apartment.

29. We should _____ things _____ before the
    inspector arrives.

30. When she discovered her husband was cheating on her, she
    _____ immediately.

Answer Key

1. remove all unnecessary items from; put in order

2. leave an area

3. remove any unnecessary or inappropriate items from; put in order

4. put in order

5. lower something fastened from above

6. move around in a disorderly way

7. give to others

8. tell someone to leave

9. slow down; bring to an end

10. steal something

11. register; indicate one's presence

12. indicate that one is leaving by signing one's name

13. leave one alone, stop nagging

14. cause not to operate or function

15. make a place secure by locking doors and setting alarms

16. get off her back

17. wind down

18. cleaned out

19. signed out

20. made off with

21. clean (everything) off

22. lock (this building) up

23. sign in

24. takes off

25. passed on

26. milled around

27. pull down

28. shut off

29. tidy (things) up

30. sent him packing

21 On the Computer

Match each word or phrase to its meaning:

1. grow out of   stop working or moving

2. be through   cause one to move less quickly

3. settle for   copy onto a disk

4. slow down   allow to continue operating; not turn off

5. go back over   register or make a record in a computer that one is about to use it

6. calm down   use to the fullest extent; use up

7. freeze up   publish; release for public use

8. back up   relax; avoid getting upset

9. wait until   turn off; stop from operating

10. come out   have no more use for something; move on to something else

11. leave on   remain inactive or refrain from doing something until something specific happens

12. shut down   start a computer

13. boot up   the initial programming a computer does internally to prepare itself for use

14. log on to   not ask for more; agree to take what one has

15. warm up   review something

Can you figure out the meanings of the italicized words in the following passages?

Conversation One:

GREG: I've *grown out of* this computer. I need one with more memory and more speed.

LAURA: This is the third computer you've *been through* this year. Shouldn't you *settle for* what you have?

GREG: Never. I won't let a machine *slow* me *down*.

Conversation Two:

VANCE: I *went back over* the manual and I still couldn't find the instructions on how to import data from one application to another.

JEANNIE: *Calm down.* Just try to fool around a bit. The worse that can happen is that the computer might *freeze up*.

VANCE: Then I'll have to call in the technician—for the fourth time this morning.

JEANNIE: Well, your only other alternative is to *wait until* they *come out with* a revised manual.

Short Talk:

Many people *leave* their computers *on* twenty-fours a day; they never *shut* them *down*. This makes their work more efficient, since they never have to *boot up* or *log on* to the system. They never have to *wait for* the computer to *warm up*. Everything is ready to use. However, if there is a power surge or a power failure, the user risks losing some data that may be impossible to reconstruct. That's why software manufacturers recommend that users *back up* their work every few hours.

Fill in the blanks to complete the sentences:

16. Roger was so furious after he lost all his work on the computer that it took him hours to _____.

17. That author is always _____ with a new book.

18. Let's try _____ both computers one more time.

19. According to our records, you _____ to Steve's computer at 6 o'clock last night.

20. Be sure to _____ your test before you hand it in for correction.

21. He's _____ four tutors and he still doesn't understand geometry.

22. Please don't _____ any of the appliances ___ when you leave the house.

23. I like to play it safe and _____ my work every few hours.

24. He realized he had _____ his obsession with tennis when he no longer wanted to play.

25. The copier won't make copies until it _____.

26. You'll have to _____ here _____ a tow truck comes for your car.

27. I asked for $1,000, and I won't _____ a penny less.

28. Every time this computer program _____, I lose valuable production time.

29. The slightest distraction will _____ him _____ when he's doing something he doesn't really want to do.

30. The Health Department had to _____ the diner _____ due to unsanitary conditions.

Answer Key

1. have no more use for something; move on to something else

2. use to the fullest extent; use up

3. not ask for more; agree to take what one has

4. cause one to move less quickly

5. review something

6. relax; avoid getting upset

7. stop working or moving

8. copy onto a disk

9. remain inactive or refrain from doing something until something specific happens

10. publish; release for public use

11. allow to continue operating; not turn off

12. turn off; stop from operating

13. start a computer

14. register or make a record in a computer that one is about to use it

15. the internal programming a computer initially does to prepare itself for use

16. calm down

17. coming out

18. booting up

19. logged on

20. go back over

21. been through

22. leave (any of the appliances) on

23. back up

24. grown out of

25. warms up

26. wait (here) until

27. settle for

28. freezes up

29. slow (him) down

30. shut (the diner) down

22 At a Hotel

Match each word or phrase to its meaning:

1. book into   complain loudly

2. make a scene   serve

3. look after   hitting, such as a door, to announce one's presence

4. nail down   register with

5. wait on   have casual conversation with

6. send up   leave a place, as a hotel

7. knock at   care for; help

8. let in   ask about; get information regarding

9. check into   delay

10. inquire about   make a reservation for

11. chat with   looking through many things to find something specific

12. search through   move downstairs

13. check out   allow to enter

14. hold on   bring to; dispatch to

15. come down   fasten securely so as to make immovable

Can you figure out the meanings of the italicized words in the following passages?

Conversation One:

ANASTASIA: My travel agent *booked* me *into* the Ritz Hotel, which is really expensive. I'm so annoyed.

CHARLES: Don't *make a scene* about it! The service will be great. Enjoy it.

ANASTASIA: I'm sure they know how to *look after* guests, but I've heard they're cautious. All the ashtrays are *nailed down*.

Conversation Two:

LADY WINDSOR: Hello, Room Service? I've been waiting for my meal for over an hour. Must I *come down* and fix it myself, or is someone going to *wait on* me as I requested?

MR. SYKES: I apologize for the *holdup*. It was *sent up* to your room ten minutes ago.

LADY WINDSOR: Well, it isn't here yet. Just a minute . . . some one's *knocking at* the door. I'll *let* him *in*.

MR. SYKES: Enjoy your breakfast, ma'am.

Short Talk:

When you *check into* a hotel, the staff should be expecting you. When you introduce yourself, they should use your name, welcome you to the hotel, and *inquire about* your trip. As they *chat with* you, they should be *searching through* the records for your reservation. When they have located your reservation, they should confirm your departure date and remind you of the daily rate. Then, there will be no surprise when you *check out*.

Fill in the blanks to complete the sentences:

16. As hotels can't _____ everything _____, they hire security personnel to keep an eye on their property.

17. I think I hear someone _____ the door.

18. My secretary _____ us _____ the Berkshire Hotel.

19. Our staff will _____ your mother while she is with us here in the nursing home.

20. As we _____ the Seaside Hotel, we were offered a senior citizen discount.

21. I had that memo _____ to your office hours ago.

22. We were _____ by the finest staff in New York at the expensive restaurant.

23. If we don't _____ by 11 A.M., we'll have to pay for another night.

24. We _____ our new neighbor today when we met in the corner store.

25. The police _____ her whereabouts last night.

26. I've _____ the classified ads and couldn't find any Help Wanted ads for bakers.

27. The owners wouldn't _____ me _____ until I produced a valid ID.

28. The guest _____ when she found out how much the room cost.

29. The waiter was _____ with his orders because of an accident in the kitchen.

30. After you get dressed, _____ to the dining room for breakfast.

Success with American Idioms

Answer Key

1. make a reservation for
2. complain loudly
3. care for; help
4. fasten securely so as to make immovable
5. serve
6. bring to; dispatch to
7. hitting, such as a door, to announce one's presence
8. allow to enter
9. register with
10. ask about; get information regarding
11. have casual conversation with
12. looking through many to find something specific
13. leave a place, as a hotel
14. wait (a minute)
15. move downstairs
16. nail (everything) down
17. knocking at
18. booked (us) into
19. look after
20. checked into
21. sent up
22. waited on
23. check out
24. chatted with
25. inquired about
26. searched through
27. let (me) in
28. made a scene
29. held up
30. come down

23 Neighborhoods

Match each word or phrase to its meaning:

1. insist on   improve; enhance

2. take care of   improve conditions; restore to earlier, better condition

3. butt into   exist

4. keep up   be at odds with

5. build up   attend to

6. fall apart   not get involved with; not get into

7. move in   prevent from, stop

8. turn around   sit or stand around with no real purpose

9. hang out   settle oneself into a particular place

10. be around   maintain

11. keep from   break down; deteriorate

12. stay out of   move forward despite obstacles or resistance

13. move into   demand and not waiver from

14. press ahead   enter; settle into

15. argue against   meddle in; interfere

Can you figure out the meanings of the italicized words in the following passages?

Conversation One:

CRAIG: I'm going to *insist on* your mowing your lawn and *taking* better *care of* your garden.

LYNETTE: Who do you think you are? What gives you the right *butt into* my affairs?

CRAIG: I'd like you to try harder to *keep up* appearances. It's better for the neighborhood.

Conversation Two:

WENDY: This neighborhood has really been *built up*. When I was here years ago, it was almost a slum.

SEAN: Right. Everything was *falling apart,* but young people *moved in* and *turned* the neighborhood *around.* Now, so many trendy shops have opened up.

WENDY: I've noticed a lot of teenagers *hanging out* on the corner. They seem to like the fact that there *are* so many fast food places *around.*

SEAN: At least the food *keeps* the kids *from* getting involved in crime. They seem to be *staying out of* trouble.

Short Talk:

When newcomers *move into* an old, dying neighborhood, they often *press ahead* with changes that the current residents are reluctant to accept. Change is always threatening, but a prosperous community is a safe one. Security and prosperity are two qualities that no one can *argue against.*

Fill in the blanks to complete the sentences:

16. I don't think anyone here would _____ funding research into solar technology.

17. Don't _____ his efforts to help these orphans; it's really none of your business.

18. The boss _____ taking us all out to a celebratory lunch.

19. It is vital that we _____ our image while the campaign is still on.

20. They _____ with their intention to strike despite terrific resistance.

21. Excessive taxation would tend to _____ new businesses _____ opening up.

22. The new human resources director really _____ employee morale _____ with her upbeat attitude.

23. Our garage is 40 years old and starting to _____.

24. If we can _____ your popularity, you'll have a better chance at knocking out the competition.

25. There _____ more than 15 churches _____ this town.

26. The snooty neighbors kicked up a fuss when the loud-mouthed family _____.

27. Until the new town gym was built, the teenagers always _____ in the parking lot.

28. My parents _____ a big house when they retired.

29. If we're going to _____ debt, we're going to have to stick to our budget.

30. Please _____ my cat while I'm gone.

Success with American Idioms

Answer Key

1. demand and not waiver from
2. attend to
3. meddle in; interfere
4. maintain
5. improve; enhance
6. break down; deteriorate
7. enter; settle into
8. improve conditions; restore to earlier better condition
9. sit or stand around with no real purpose
10. exist
11. prevent from, stop
12. not get involved with; not get into
13. integrate oneself in; settle into
14. move forward despite obstacles or resistance
15. be at odds with
16. argue against
17. butt into
18. insisted on
19. keep up
20. pressed ahead
21. keep (new businesses) from
22. turned (employee morale) around
23. fall apart
24. build up
25. are (more than 15 churches) around
26. moved in
27. hung out
28. moved into
29. stay out of
30. take care of

24 Creatures of Habit

Match each word or phrase to its meaning:

1. stick to — discard; free oneself from
2. run up and down — persist
3. get out of — no longer be friendly with; end relations with
4. keep at — be worthwhile
5. pay off — overdo something; exaggerate; get overemotional
6. see in — perceive to be attractive or desirable
7. keep on — come up with ideas
8. run around — stay; not deviate from
9. figure out — take away
10. disapprove of — move around
11. get rid of — persist; not give up
12. disassociate from — determine
13. get carried away — go up an incline and then come back down
14. think up — find fault with
15. cart off — no longer continue to do or be

Can you figure out the meanings of the italicized words in the following passages?

Conversation One:

CARLOS: How long have you been *sticking to* your exercise routine?

EVELIA: I've *kept at* it for almost a year. Every morning at 7 A.M. I *run up and down* the hill behind my house. I'm afraid to stop, because I might get out of the habit.

CARLOS: Well, *keep at* it. All the hard work is *paying off.* You look great.

Conversation Two:

VICKY: I don't know what you *see in* her.

PAUL: She's a very disciplined woman, and I need someone to help me *keep on* a narrow path.

VICKY: There's nothing wrong with *running around* without a purpose.

PAUL: I disagree. I want to establish a goal and *figure out* the shortest path to reach it. But I can't do it alone.

Short Talk:

Even though you may *disapprove of* a friend's bad habits, it is almost impossible to get them to *get rid of* these habits. People are quite fond of their way of doing things. If a habit like drumming one's fingers on the table or rattling keys in a pocket irritates you, *think up* ways to *disassociate* yourself *from* this person. Don't *get carried away* and start yelling "You're driving me crazy!!" You'll be labelled as the one who should be *carted off* to a mental hospital.

Fill in the blanks to complete the sentences:

16. The town council _____ putting another high-rise in the downtown area.

17. I don't understand what you _____ this particular line of work—to me it seems dreadfully boring.

18. You can't just _____ being unemployed forever.

19. With our deficit, it will be difficult to _____ how to break even.

20. _____ your exercise program and I'm sure you'll feel better in a few weeks.

21. I _____ shape when I took that desk job.

22. They _____ him _____ to the asylum when he tried to jump off the bridge.

23. He tends to _____ when he talks about his fishing trip.

24. I've tried to _____ the termites at least four different times.

25. He decided to _____ himself _____ the negative people in his life to make himself feel better.

26. His only exercise is _____ the stairs at work.

27. When the boss promoted me to a higher level position, I knew all my efforts had finally _____.

28. This congressman has a real talent for _____ ways to attract voters.

29. If we just _____ it, I know we can reach our fundraising goal.

30. He has a difficult time _____ his attention _____ his work.

Answer Key

1. persist; not give up
2. go up an incline and then come back down
3. no longer continue to do or be
4. persist
5. be worthwhile
6. perceive to be attractive or desirable
7. stay; not deviate from
8. move around
9. determine
10. not argue with; find fault with
11. discard; free oneself from
12. no longer be friendly with; end relations with
13. overdo something; exaggerate; get overemotional
14. come up with ideas
15. take away

16. disapproved of
17. see in
18. run around
19. figure out
20. stick to
21. got out of
22. carted (him) off
23. get carried away
24. get rid of
25. disassociate (himself) from
26. running up and down
27. paid off
28. thinking up
29. keep at
30. keeping (his attention) on

25 Temper Tantrums

Match each word or phrase to its meaning:

1. tell off   leave; get moving

2. block out   substitute with

3. do without   become public knowledge; become known

4. shut up   stop talking

5. take a hike   discard; cause to cease to exist

6. flare up   discover

7. help out   get by without

8. foul up   fill with clouds; become less bright

9. find out   ruin; louse up

10. do away with   shut out

11. get out   explode in anger

12. make up for   assist; be of assistance

13. mail out   speak to angrily

14. cloud over   send or distribute via the postal system

15. blow up   to become suddenly excited or angry

Can you figure out the meanings of the italicized words in the following passages?

Conversation One:

STUART: Why don't you draw the curtains? If you *block out* the light, you'll be able to sleep better.

BERNICE: I can *do without* your advice. Just *shut up* and *take a hike*, will you?

STUART: There's no reason to *flare up*. I'm just trying to *help you out*. Why are you always *telling* me *off* for no reason?

Conversation Two:

CANDACE: Well, you really seem to have *fouled* this project *up*.

ARTHUR: You'll *find out* that my way is the right way.

CANDACE: I've been trying to *do away with* your job for a year now. When this news *gets out*, you and your job will be history.

ARTHUR: What you lack in brains, you *make up for* in aggression. If I were you, I'd start *mailing out* my résumé, because you're the one who'll need a new job when I'm through with you.

Short Talk:

When the sky *clouds over*, we tend to become more gloomy. In the winter, when days are shorter, our tempers also become shorter and we *blow up* at the slightest provocation. Nothing seems right. We can't *find* pleasure *in* anything. Fortunately, spring is just around the corner to lift our spirits.

Fill in the blanks to complete the sentences:

16. I try to _____ the noise at my office by using ear phones.

17. He got angry at his friend's incessant chatter and finally told him to _____.

18. Roger _____ at his wife when he found out she had thrown out his favorite shirt.

19. Nothing can _____ all the heirlooms she lost in the fire.

20. We're _____ the invitations to our Open House tomorrow.

21. The teacher _____ her student for not doing his homework.

22. I can't afford to _____ this presentation to these prospective clients.

23. Hopefully the sky won't _____ during our outdoor wedding.

24. The policemen told all the onlookers to _____; there was nothing for them to see at the accident scene.

25. I don't know how we _____ a dishwasher this long.

26. He _____ at other people only when he doesn't get a good night's sleep.

27. After you move in, let me know if I can _____ you _____ in any way.

28. He soon _____ that he should have put more money aside for taxes.

29. You'll have to _____ if you can't control yourself.

30. Some day, the government will _____ income tax.

Answer Key

1. speak to angrily
2. shut out
3. get by without
4. stop talking
5. leave; get moving
6. become suddenly excited or angry
7. assist; be of assistance
8. ruin; louse up
9. discover
10. discard; cause to cease to exist
11. become public knowledge; become known
12. substitute with
13. send or distribute via the postal system
14. fill with clouds; become less bright
15. explode in anger
16. block out
17. shut up
18. blew up
19. make up for
20. mailing out
21. told off
22. foul up
23. cloud over
24. take a hike
25. did without
26. flares up
27. help (you) out
28. found out
29. get out
30. do away with

26 Having a Good Time

Match each word or phrase to its meaning:

1.	get a lot out of	restrain oneself
2.	walk through	encourage, demand
3.	push for	reach readily for
4.	come along	be in the company of and friendly with
5.	hold back	stroll in
6.	get to	sitting around
7.	cry for	find out about from others
8.	hear of	be lazy, stop working hard
9.	be content with	stop working and sit down
10.	jump at	learn much from
11.	slack off	arrive at
12.	get away from	shed tears about
13.	pal around	remove oneself from
14.	end up	be satisfied with
15.	kick back	accompany; join

Can you figure out the meanings of the italicized words in the following passages?

Conversation One:

ERNEST: I really *got a lot out of* that lecture on nature.

SARAH: Me, too. I never knew that a *walk through* the woods could be so educational. Can I *come along* next time you have this class?

ERNEST: Sure! I'm going to *push for* these lectures to become a regular feature of our curriculum.

Conversation Two:

ELIZA: Don't *hold back*. If you want to cry, just let the tears flow.

HANK: When I *get to* that point, I'll let you know.

ELIZA: When I'm really happy, I sob like a baby. You know the expression "to *cry for* joy"?

HANK: Yes. I've *heard of* it. In my case, would you *be content with* a big smile?

Short Talk:

If someone offered you a two-week paid vacation, anywhere you wanted to go, would you *jump at* the chance? Or is your idea of a good time to *slack off* work and watch TV at home? Would you rather *get away from* it all on a tropical island or would you rather *pal around* with your buddies? Whether you *end up* in a resort or on your neighbor's couch, you can still have the time of your life. All you have to do is *kick back* and relax.

Fill in the blanks to complete the sentences:

16. It's probably best not to _____ with the boss too much; it could make your coworkers jealous.

17. At seven o'clock every night I _____ and watch the news.

18. I _____ the Time Management Seminar; I left with ten pages of notes.

19. She _____ joy when she heard that she won the sweepstakes.

20. He _____ the park last night after work.

21. Doctors and nurses sometimes need to _____ all the pain they deal with on a day-to-day basis.

22. The union members _____ the pay increase that the management offered them.

23. Our boss is _____ raises for our entire department.

24. I don't think we'll _____ the last chapter in the book today.

25. You're definitely welcome to _____ with us to the museum.

26. We _____ somewhere in Jersey City, about 25 miles off course.

27. Jerry is really _____ at work these days; I'm afraid he might get fired.

28. I haven't _____ anyone having problems with the copy machine lately; it must be fixed.

29. He _____ the chance to apply for the job.

30. Though I was upset at my coworker, I _____ myself _____ until I could speak calmly and rationally.

Answer Key

1. learn much from
2. stroll in
3. encourage; demand
4. accompany; join
5. restrain oneself
6. arrive at; reach
7. shed tears about
8. find out about from others
9. be satisfied with
10. reach readily for
11. be lazy; stop working hard
12. remove oneself from
13. be in the company of and friendly with
14. arrive at
15. stop working and sit down

16. pal around
17. kick back
18. got a lot out of
19. cried for
20. walked through
21. get away from
22. were content with
23. pushing for
24. get to
25. come along
26. ended up
27. slacking off
28. heard of
29. jumped at
30. held (myself) back

27 Under the Weather

Match each word or phrase to its meaning:

1. shake off   expect a good thing to happen

2. be flat on one's   spread from one to another
   back

3. ask after   ill, feeling bad

4. rush back   inhale and exhale

5. under the weather   cause to be in bed, as by an illness

6. look forward to   return quickly

7. come down with   slow down, relax

8. breathe in and out   be free from; get rid of

9. go around   expect

10. take off   inquire about

11. lay up   be overly concerned about

12. worry about   have the beginning signs of, as in an
                                 illness

13. take it easy   make happy; brighten one's outlook

14. bargain for   not work

15. cheer up   be sick in bed

Can you figure out the meanings of the italicized words in the following passages?

Conversation One:

DOMINIC: I can't seem to *shake off* this cold. I've been *flat on my back* for a week.

EVE: Everyone is *asking after* you, but don't *rush back* to work; we know you're *under the weather*.

DOMINIC: You don't know how much I'm *looking forward to* being cured.

Conversation Two:

JOANNE: I think I'm *coming down with* something. My throat hurts and I'm really tired. And I have to *breathe in and out* through my mouth.

LEON: The flu is *going around*. Sounds like you have the symptoms.

JOANNE: This is the worst possible time to get sick. I have an important meeting this week.

LEON: Nothing is more important than your health. Why don't you *take* a few days *off*? Maybe you'll feel better when it's time for your meeting.

Short Talk:

If you are *laid up* with an illness, you should not think about anything but improving your health. If you begin to *worry about* your work or family responsibilities, the stress will prolong your illness and *slow down* your recovery. You'll spend more time in bed than you *bargained for*. So *cheer up* and enjoy the change in pace as you *take it easy* at home. You'll be back at work soon enough.

Fill in the blanks to complete the sentences:

16. My secretary has the flu and has been _____ with a fever for over a week now.

17. There doesn't seem to be a medicine that can cure the particular strain of flu that's been _____.

18. Even though I didn't get my own office, I should _____ —I did get a raise, after all.

19. The doctor said I just needed to _____ during my workout routine to avoid overtiring myself.

20. There's no need to _____ losing the vacation time you earned.

21. No matter what I do, I can't _____ this cold.

22. The messenger _____ to pick up the letter he had forgotten.

23. I never _____ such a pleasant working environment, but I love it!

24. He feels like he's _____ the same cold you had last week.

25. I _____ to my vacation in the Bahamas next week.

26. I'd love to go the convention, but I can't afford to _____ any more time _____ work.

27. The nurse asked me to _____ while she listened with her stethoscope.

28. Our janitor has been _____ for weeks with pneumonia.

29. Something must be wrong with me; for three days I've been feeling _____.

30. The patients have been _____ you, Dr. Barnes.

Answer Key

1. be free from; get rid of
2. be sick in bed
3. inquire about
4. return quickly
5. ill, feeling bad
6. expect a good thing to happen
7. have the beginning signs of, as in an illness
8. inhale and exhale
9. spread from one to another
10. not work
11. cause to be in bed, as by an illness
12. be overly concerned about
13. slow down, relax
14. expect
15. make happy; brighten one's outlook
16. flat on her back
17. going around
18. cheer up
19. take it easy
20. worry about
21. shake off
22. rushed back
23. bargained for
24. coming down with
25. look forward
26. take (any more time) off
27. breathe in and out
28. laid up
29. under the weather
30. asking after

28 Old Clothes

Match each word or phrase to its meaning:

1. wear out   recover; feel better about

2. give away   not let go of; keep in one's possession

3. write off   learn about and keep pace with

4. get over   see; find; notice

5. wear through   sort out to find certain items

6. rip off   use clothes so often or so long that the fabric weakens or tears

7. throw out   search for

8. keep up with   decide something or someone is useless

9. weed out   return; show up again

10. attach to   create hole by friction because of being used so long or so often, as with an item of clothing

11. hang on to   put in the garbage, discard

12. come back   cause to return

13. run across   cheat

14. hunt for   to bind in a personal or emotional way

15. bring back   let someone have for free

Can you figure out the meanings of the italicized words in the following passages?

Conversation One:

THEO: I've almost *worn out* this shirt.

ELLEN: Why don't you just *give* it *away*?

THEO: It's my favorite shirt. Giving it away would be like *writing off* an old friend. I'd never *get over* losing it.

Conversation Two:

BELINDA: I thought this spot was where the shirt had *worn through*, but it turns out to be just a stain.

FLOYD: It's an old stain, isn't it? You could take it to the cleaners if it were fresh.

BELINDA: Well, I won't *throw* it *out*—I like that shirt even with a stain. And I'm sure to be *ripped off* if I buy a new one like it. They're ridiculously expensive now.

Short Talk:

Even people who buy new clothes every season and try to *keep up with* the latest fashions find it difficult to *weed* their old clothes *out* of their closets. They become *attached to* a particular shirt, blouse, pair of pants, or belt. Even though it may not fit, the color is faded, or the style is old, they *hang on to* it for sentimental reasons. Who knows? Maybe it will *come back* into style. Even if it doesn't, it doesn't hurt anyone sitting by itself at the back of the closet. And when you *run across* it while *hunting for* a missing sock, it will *bring back* memories of the days when you wore that piece of clothing.

Fill in the blanks to complete the sentences:

16. He never _____ the loss of his dog.

17. Teenager don't seem to have a problem _____ with the latest hair trends.

18. She became very _____ the dress she had worn to the prom.

19. The smell of the coffee _____ thoughts of last year's vacation in Brazil.

20. I didn't _____ anything that really appealed to me in the clothing store.

21. The material on the lawn chairs is all _____.

22. I haven't talked to Kevin in years. I _____ him _____ after he never returned my calls.

23. I'll _____ the files that have been around for more than ten years.

24. I've been _____ a belt to go with this suit.

25. You should _____ this jewelry, because it will be a collector's item someday.

26. These hats are so ugly that you've can't _____ them _____.

27. The elbows on this shirt have _____.

28. We _____ all the books damaged by the flood.

29. The salesmen _____ her _____ when he sold her a fake Rolex watch for $500.

30. Trends in fashion always _____ again and again.

Answer Key

1. use clothes so often or so long that the fabric weakens or tears

2. let someone have for free

3. decide something is useless

4. recover; feel better about

5. create hole by friction because of being used so long or so often, as with an item of clothing

6. cheat

7. put in the garbage, discard

8. learn about and keep pace with

9. sort out to find certain items

10. to bind in a personal or emotional way

11. not let go of; keep in one's possession

12. return; show up again

13. see; find; notice

14. search for

15. cause to return

16. got over

17. keeping up

18. attached to

19. brought back

20. run across

21. worn out

22. wrote (him) off

23. weed out

24. hunting for

25. hang on to

26. give (them) away

27. worn through

28. threw out

29. ripped (her) off

30. come back

29 Changing Your Mind

Match each word or phrase to its meaning:

1. come around	betray; lose one's ideals
2. count on	accept
3. size up	lose opportunity to do
4. pass off	admit one was wrong about something one said; retract
5. take up	conclude; consider
6. cross over	become glassy-eyed or have a fixed, lifeless expression
7. mix with	fall asleep
8. lose out on	rely on; assume
9. sell out	change over or to
10. dawn on	switch sides; move beyond
11. take back	join; bring together
12. switch over	have same opinion
13. glaze over	eventually agree with; eventually become aware of
14. doze off	occur to; realize
15. agree with	cause oneself to be thought of in a certain way, though it isn't a true picture

Can you figure out the meanings of the italicized words in the following passages?

Conversation One:

NIGEL: He'll *come around* to my way of thinking.

TESSA: Don't *count on* it. He *sized* you *up* as a dilettante long ago.

NIGEL: I take that as a compliment. I've never tried to *pass* myself *off* as anything else.

Conversation Two:

TESSA: I'm ready to *take* you *up on* your offer to explain why I should *cross over* to your political party.

NIGEL: I've changed my mind. I don't want to *mix* my politics *with* our friendship.

TESSA: And I don't want to *lose out on* an opportunity to learn why you *sold out* and went over to the opposition.

NIGEL: Has it *dawned on* you that you have a closed mind? I think you should *take back* that obnoxious comment.

Short Talk:

Have you ever tried to get someone to *switch over* to your point of view and watched their eyes begin to *glaze over* as they begin to *doze off*? People have to be receptive to new ideas in order to accept them. Some people are stubborn; they fix an idea in their heads and nothing can budge it. There is no problem with this attitude if these people *agree with* you. Other people change their minds with each new opinion they hear. There is no problem with this attitude either, so long as the last opinion they hear is yours!

Fill in the blanks to complete the sentences:

16. I'm going to _____ you _____ on your challenge to swim across the English Channel.

17. You want to be sure not to _____ ammonia _____ bleach.

18. When Lola found out that George had never left his house that night, she had to _____ her accusation that he had smashed into her car.

19. John _____ when the professor kept using words he didn't understand.

20. Karen _____ the scholarship because she missed its application deadline.

21. I _____ his business and decided it wouldn't be a good idea to invest in it at this time.

22. In a work environment, there's a certain point you don't want to _____ in relationships.

23. It never _____ him that he could be fired for insubordination.

24. He _____ his siblings just to get the inheritance.

25. It was only a matter of time before the son _____ to his father's viewpoint.

26. The Wilsons finally _____ the decorators about which color scheme would best suit the living room.

27. Don't _____ the caterers to bring all the utensils.

28. When his eyes _____, I knew he wasn't really interested in my lecture.

29. She tried to _____ herself _____ as a reporter at the press conference.

30. I _____ to the Republican party after discovering that I agreed more with their policies.

Success with American Idioms

Answer Key

1. eventually agree with; eventually become aware of
2. rely on; assume
3. conclude; consider
4. cause oneself to be thought of in a certain way, though it isn't a true picture
5. accept
6. switch sides; move beyond
7. join; bring together
8. lose opportunity to do
9. betray; lose one's ideals
10. occur to; realize
11. admit one was wrong (about something one said); retract
12. change over or to
13. become glassy-eyed or have a fixed, lifeless expression
14. fall asleep
15. concur; have same opinion
16. take (you) up
17. mix (ammonia) with
18. take back
19. dozed off
20. lost out on
21. sized up
22. cross over
23. dawned on
24. sold out
25. came around
26. agreed with
27. count on
28. glazed over
29. pass (herself) off
30. switched over

Match each word or phrase to its meaning:

1. count toward   take joy or pleasure in

2. warm up   take all the money out; withdraw all funds

3. get on   not participate in

4. call out   enter forcefully

5. empty out   board; set oneself onto

6. hand out   give away for nothing in return

7. shell out   participate in; be part of

8. sit on the sidelines   contribute to

9. pick oneself up   contribute; help

10. make a difference   involve oneself with; participate in; become one of

11. get in with   exercise to get the blood moving more rapidly

12. join in   give away; distribute for free

13. pitch in   survive

14. delight in   change the situation for the better

15. pull through   say aloud, as over a loudspeaker

Can you figure out the meanings of the italicized words in the following passages?

Conversation One:

REX: Every mile we ride *counts toward* our goal of raising one million dollars. Our sponsors have pledged one dollar for every mile.

CAITLIN: We'd better *warm up* before we *get on* those bikes.

REX: Yes, because when they *call out* the start of the race, we have to be off and running.

Conversation Two:

GLADYS: I *emptied out* my bank account to give money to the homeless.

MARVIN: I hope you left enough to pay your rent, or you'll be living on the street yourself.

GLADYS: I'm exaggerating, but I think we should *hand out* as much as we can spare.

MARVIN: I'm donating my time in a food kitchen. I don't have any spare cash to *shell out* at the moment.

Short Talk:

Do you find yourself often *sitting on the sidelines*? Why not *pick yourself up* and do something? *Get in with* the crowd. *Join in* the fun. *Pitch in* and help. There are thousands of volunteer groups around the country that need your support. You can *delight in* seeing your participation in a reading program improve the reading scores in a local elementary school. You can help others *pull through* difficult emotional times. You can work with the community and help them *pull together* to achieve some civic goal. In short, you can *make a difference*. All you have to do is volunteer.

Fill in the blanks to complete the sentences:

16. Even though she knew she didn't have a great voice, she _____ when she heard everyone singing.

17. She managed to _____ some very tough times and is doing well now.

18. Your name will be _____ when it's time to receive your award.

19. Cartons of food were _____ throughout the night to hungry people.

20. The coach's pep talk obviously _____— his team played well and won the game.

21. I'm sorry, but I can't _____ any more money for this charity.

22. Maybe his office will _____ some funds for the research department.

23. This $300 _____ the $5,000 I owe you for the repair of the garage.

24. Stop _____ and get in here and help us.

25. I was told that it's good to _____ before running.

26. I _____ my savings account to go on this trip.

27. We _____ our motorcycles and drove across the country.

28. He _____ himself ____ and got a job this afternoon.

29. George will never _____ the martini drinking crowd; he's simply too casual.

30. We all _____ seeing our school win the game.

Answer Key

1. contribute to

2. exercise to get the blood moving more rapidly

3. board; set oneself onto

4. say aloud, as over a loud-speaker

5. take all the money out; withdraw all funds

6. give away; distribute for free

7. give away for nothing in return

8. not participate in

9. set in motion; cause to do something

10. enthusiastically enter

11. involve oneself with; participate in; become one of

12. participate in; be part of

13. contribute; help

14. take joy or pleasure in

15. survive

16. joined in

17. pull through

18. called out

19. handed out

20. made a difference

21. shell out

22. pitch in

23. counts toward

24. sitting on the sidelines

25. warm up

26. emptied out

27. got on

28. picked (himself) up

29. get in with

30. delighted in

Index

Success with American Idioms

About KAPLAN
Educational Centers

Kaplan Educational Centers is one of the nation's premier education companies, providing individuals with a full range of resources to achieve their educational and career goals. Kaplan, celebrating its 60th anniversary, is a wholly-owned subsidiary of The Washington Post Company.

TEST PREPARATION & ADMISSIONS

Kaplan's nationally-recognized test prep courses cover more than 20 standardized tests, including entrance exams for secondary school, college and graduate school as well as foreign language and professional licensing exams. In addition, Kaplan offers private tutoring and comprehensive, one-to-one admissions and application advice for students applying to graduate school.

SCORE! EDUCATIONAL CENTERS

SCORE! after-school learning centers help students in grades K-8 build academic skills, confidence and goal-setting skills in a motivating, sports-oriented environment. Kids use a cutting-edge, interactive curriculum that continually assesses and adapts to their academic needs and learning style. Enthusiastic Academic Coaches serve as positive role models, creating a high-energy atmosphere where learning is exciting and fun for kids. With nearly 40 centers today, SCORE! continues to open new centers nationwide.

KAPLAN LEARNING SERVICES

Kaplan Learning Services provides customized assessment, education and training programs to K-12 schools, universities and businesses to help students and employees reach their educational and career goals.

KAPLAN INTERNATIONAL

Kaplan serves international students and professionals in the U.S. through Access America, a series of intensive English language programs, and LCP

International Institute, a leading provider of intensive English language programs at on-campus centers in California, Washington and New York. Kaplan and LCP offer specialized services to sponsors including placement at top American universities, fellowship management, academic monitoring and reporting and financial administration.

KAPLOAN

Students can get key information and advice about educational loans for college and graduate school through **KapLoan** (Kaplan Student Loan Information Program). Through an affiliation with one of the nation's largest student loan providers, **KapLoan** helps direct students and their families through the often bewildering financial aid process.

KAPLAN PUBLISHING

Kaplan Books, a joint imprint with Simon & Schuster, publishes books in test preparation, admissions, education,career development and life skills; Kaplan and *Newsweek* jointly publish the highly successful guides, **How to Get Into College** and **How to Choose a Career & Graduate School**. SCORE! and *Newsweek* have teamed up to publish **How to Help Your Child Suceed in School**.

Kaplan InterActive delivers award-winning, high quality educational products and services including Kaplan's best-selling **Higher Score** test-prep software and sites on the internet **(http://www.kaplan.com)** and America Online. Kaplan and Cendant Software are jointly developing, marketing and distributing educational software for the kindergarten through twelfth grade retail and school markets.

KAPLAN CAREER SERVICES

Kaplan helps students and graduates find jobs through Kaplan Career Services, the leading provider of career fairs in North America. The division includes **Crimson & Brown Associates**, the nation's leading diversity recruiting and publishing firm, and **The Lendman Group and Career Expo**, both of which help clients identify highly sought-after technical personnel and sales and marketing professionals.

COMMUNITY OUTREACH

Kaplan provides educational resources to thousands of financially disadvantaged students annually, working closely with educational institutions, not-for-profit groups, government agencies and other grass roots organizations on a variety of national and local support programs. Also, Kaplan centers enrich local communities by employing high school, college and graduate students, creating valuable work experiences for vast numbers of young people each year.

Paying for college just got easier...

KapLoan*, the Kaplan Student Loan Information Program, is a free service designed to guide you through the financial aid process.

KapLoan will send you a FREE booklet with valuable financial aid information and connect you with one of the nation's largest student loan providers. With KapLoan, you'll receive personalized guidance through the financial aid process and access to some of the least expensive educational loans available.

- **The Federal Stafford Loan**—Eligible students can borrow various amounts depending on their year in college. Loan amounts range from $2,625-$5,500 for dependent students and $6,625-$10,500 for independent students.

- **The Federal Parent Loan for Undergraduate Students (PLUS)**—Eligible parents may borrow up to the total cost of education, less other financial aid received.

Make the most of your financial aid opportunities.

The Kaplan Student Loan Information Program

Contact KapLoan today!

1-888-KAP-LOAN
www.kaploan.com

Give mom something *new* to brag about.

With 60 years of proven success getting students into the schools of their choice, we're the chosen leader in test prep. Just ask anyone who's taken Kaplan. They can easily be found at a grad school near you.

Classes are filling fast, so call today to reserve a seat.

1-800-KAP-TEST
www.kaplan.com